	DATE DUE		

YOU
ARE THE
PRESIDENT II
1800-1899

GREAT DECISIONS

YOU
ARE THE
PRESIDENT II
1800-1899

Nathan Aaseng

The Oliver Press, Inc.
Minneapolis

The Oliver Press, Inc.
Josiah King House
2709 Lyndale Avenue South
Minneapolis, MN 55408

Library of Congress Cataloging-in-Publication Data

Aaseng, Nathan.

You are the president II: 1800-1899 / Nathan Aaseng.

p. cm. — (Great decisions)
Includes bibliographical references and index.
ISBN 1-881508-15-3 : $14.95
1. United States—Politics and government—19th century—
Decision making—Juvenile literature. 2. United States—Foreign relations—19th century—Decision making—Juvenile literature.
3. Presidents—United States—Decision making—Juvenile literature. [1. Presidents. 2. United States—Politics and government—19th century. 3. Decision making.] I. Title. II. Series.
E743.A16 1994b
973.5—dc20   93-46308
                                                 CIP
                                                  AC

ISBN: 1-881508-15-3
Great Decisions IV
Printed in the United States of America

99 98 97 96 95 94   8 7 6 5 4 3 2 1

CONTENTS

George Washington (1732-1799), the first president of the United States, died before he could share his wisdom and experience with the nineteenth-century presidents who succeeded him.

INTRODUCTION

You are about to go back in time to become the most powerful person in the United States. You are going to decide what action will be taken to solve some of the most crucial issues in U.S. history. Your decisions will affect the lives of millions of people and perhaps even alter the course of history.

No one can make these decisions for you. You can study reports and charts and listen to expert advice until your eyes glaze over, but these experts are not the president of the United States. In the end, the final decision will be yours.

The choices are not easy, and traps and pitfalls await you. As you wrestle with these complex issues, people will be watching over your shoulder, evaluating your every move. The American people can be harsh critics, but your political opponents are even worse. They are circling like sharks, waiting for you to make even one mistake so they can move in for the kill.

The pressure of the presidency is enough to faze even the strongest individuals. Some stagger to the end of their term, counting the days until they can be rid of this horrendous responsibility. Upon leaving office, President James Buchanan declared to his successor, "If you are as happy in entering the White House as I shall feel on returning to Wheatland, you are a happy man indeed."

Welcome to the world of the president! This book puts you at the center of the United States government during the nineteenth century. You will encounter eight actual crises faced by eight different U.S. presidents. Advisers will summarize the situation for you and then present you with options. Your job is to solve each crisis by choosing one of these options.

Abraham Lincoln, who succeeded James Buchanan as president, learned that even one wrong decision could divide the nation.

The White House (pictured here in the mid-nineteenth century) has been the home to U.S. presidents since 1800, when John Adams moved in.

After you have done so, you will see what the real president did in each situation and why he made the choice he did. Then you will discover what happened as a result of that decision. Finally, to help you evaluate the wisdom of the president's choice, each chapter includes a hindsight section that—given the benefit of knowing how events unfolded—evaluates the wisdom of the president's choice.

Presidents make mistakes just like everyone else, and you will find that some of these decisions did not work out the way the presidents had planned. Perhaps you will find evidence that the choice you made would have worked better than the choice made at the time.

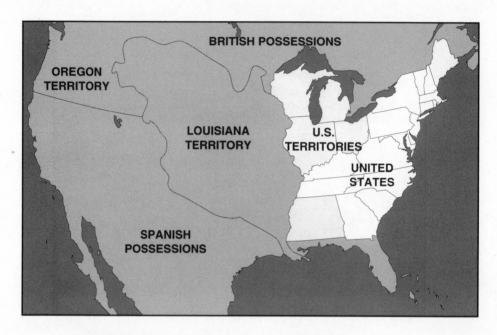

In 1800, the United States had 16 states and settlements in some of the neighboring territories, the British occupied Canada and Oregon, the Spanish controlled Florida and the Southwest, and Spain ceded the Louisiana Territory to France.

These eight crises span the nineteenth century—a time when the United States was trying to establish its place in the world. Unlike the great European powers, your nation is still relatively new; you do not have centuries of tradition to guide your steps. Most of the problems you encounter will involve charting the boundaries and the destiny of the North American continent.

Now prepare to jump back into history. Sitting back and criticizing presidential decisions is easy. But now comes the time to find out what it's like being the president who has to make those decisions!

1

NEW ORLEANS
January 1803

No location in the world poses a greater threat to the vital interests of the United States than the port of New Orleans at the base of the Mississippi River. The commerce of many of your states travels down this great waterway through New Orleans along the western edge of your borders. Should the owners of that port close it to your shipping, they could strangle the economy of the western United States.

Presently, Spain owns New Orleans, and this European country has permitted U.S. river traffic. By the terms of the Treaty of San Lorenzo, signed by the United States and Spain in 1795, Spain has allowed U.S. ships to use the port of New Orleans without paying a duty on their goods.

Recent political maneuvering among the European powers, however, has made you nervous about the situation in New Orleans. Although Spain was once a powerful nation that staked a vast claim in the Americas, its influence has faded considerably. The Spanish armies are no longer a match for the European powers of France and Great Britain and do not intimidate even a lesser power such as the United States.

Recently, the Spanish agreed to give their vast Louisiana Territory, including New Orleans, to France. At the moment, the French are preparing a large fleet to sail to the Americas to take control of their new acquisition.

Shortly after hearing this news, you received word that the very event you most feared has come to pass. In October 1802, Juan Morales, the Spanish official in charge of New Orleans, suddenly closed the port to U.S. shipping.

BACKGROUND

No one in your government knows why Morales has closed the port. He may have a legitimate reason for acting on his own authority. For example, American shippers have angered the Spanish by abusing their free-port privileges to smuggle illegal goods. Morales may be trying to crack down on that activity. Or, for some unknown reason, he may be acting on the orders of Spain or, perhaps, under orders from the incoming new masters of New Orleans—the French.

Spain has been suspiciously cozy with France in recent years. Fear is the likely reason. The Spanish are eager to stay on good terms with their powerful, aggressive neighbor. They are already hard pressed to defend their own country, much less their far-flung American outposts across the Atlantic Ocean. Spain probably hopes to gain favor with this powerful European nation by ceding their defenseless American territories to France.

While Spanish control of New Orleans presents no problems to Americans, the thought of France controlling that port alarms you. Generally, the United States has been on good terms with France, its ally in your recent war for independence from Britain. But France is no longer the champion of liberty and democracy it was a decade ago. Its current leader, Napoleon Bonaparte, is a dangerous man with an enormous ego. Your sources tell you this brilliant military leader, who heads the world's most powerful army, dreams of establishing a powerful French empire in America. This new empire, stretching from the Mississippi Valley to the Gulf of Mexico, would threaten your national security, especially if Napoleon's ambitions keep driving him to conquer more territory.

Ironically, the British stand ready to assist you in any military venture against the French. Like the Spanish, the British fear Napoleon. They would gladly let bygones be bygones with Americans if you took up arms against their archenemy. Great Britain's naval superiority combined with U.S. land forces would be unbeatable in North America. From across the Atlantic Ocean, France would have great difficulty supplying and defending its sparsely populated colonial territory against that alliance.

THE DECISION IS YOURS.

How will you respond to the Spanish closing of New Orleans and the looming French takeover of the port?

Option 1 **Negotiate to buy New Orleans from the French.**

Some of your advisers with contacts in France believe that the French might be willing to sell New Orleans for roughly $6 million. They note that Napoleon's main objective is to defeat Great Britain. He has been toying with two basic options—conquering Great Britain and its allies in Europe or defeating them by establishing a powerful colonial empire in the New World. French armies have proven nearly invincible on the European continent. However, its more powerful navy gives Great Britain a large advantage in fighting a war across the ocean, especially if the Americans join them.

Napoleon will quickly see that France stands a better chance of success if it concentrates its efforts in Europe. The more money Napoleon has to finance his armies, the better his chances of defeating Great Britain and its allies. Therefore, Napoleon may be willing to listen to a reasonable offer to purchase land that the French would have trouble holding against a British-American attack.

Although the struggling American economy can scarcely afford to pay $6 million for a city, you would not have to levy new taxes to come up with that sum. France owes the United States approximately $5 million in

Many Americans feared that France, under the leadership of Napoleon Bonaparte (1769-1821), would become a threat to the United States.

damages to American shipping by French privateers. Thus, the U.S. could raise most of the purchase money simply by cancelling the French debt.

This option also spares you the discomfort of allying yourself with Great Britain. Previous U.S. politicians have warned against forming alliances that would involve them in the wars between European powers. Many officials in the British government have not fully accepted American independence. They seek to get the United States back under British control by making the Americans as dependent as possible on Great Britain.

By avoiding a fight with France, you will spare the United States the need to accept British military aid.

Option 2 Attack the Spanish and seize New Orleans immediately.

Morales, the Spanish authority in New Orleans, has failed to follow the provisions of the Treaty of San Lorenzo. He has taken actions that gravely threaten the economic survival of the United States. No self-respecting country can tolerate such actions.

If, as many suspect, the French are behind the closing, then the national security of the United States may be at stake. If you do not take serious steps to secure the port of New Orleans, American shipping on the Mississippi River could be at the mercy of France for many years. In a sense, Spain's closure of the port has presented you with a rare opportunity. This action gives you a valid reason for seizing New Orleans and permanently eliminating one of America's nagging concerns.

The Federalists, the strongest American political party in opposition to your government, argue that the present situation leaves you only two alternatives: 1) You can negotiate to try and purchase the land and, if that fails, seize New Orleans by force, or 2) you can seize the area by force now and then negotiate. France is not likely to sell what they have so recently acquired, especially given Napoleon's dream of a New World empire. War, therefore, is the better option.

You should attack New Orleans now while Spain is still holding the port. Given Spain's weakened military state, you have at least a reasonable chance of defeating its defenses. Capturing New Orleans will enable you to negotiate with the French from a position of strength. By negotiating first, you simply give the French a chance to stall until their army arrives in full force at New Orleans. Once that happens, you may never be able to dislodge them.

Option 3 Declare war on France.

By declaring their intention to take over New Orleans, the port most vital to American business, the French have already taken hostile action against the United States. The outraged American public is crying out for you to take action.

You cannot depend on negotiations to get you anywhere with Napoleon. He is far too ambitious to sell New Orleans to you—either now or in the future. Nor will his ego allow you to remain in possession of the port of New Orleans indefinitely. It is, after all, the property of France; the Spanish are merely holding it for the

French until they arrive. The vastly superior French military forces will eventually bear down on the Americans holding their property.

For these reasons, you cannot afford to proceed cautiously. You would be far better off fighting an aggressive war against all French-occupied territory on the North American continent. Since France presents the major threat to U.S. interests, you would be wise to evict the French from the lands along your borders. You have the military advantage of being able to strike quickly at these lands while France must send its troops on a long Atlantic crossing. If you can take over all key French possessions on the North American continent, France will have difficulty regaining those possessions.

Now is the time to settle this. The United States would be foolish to challenge France by itself, but Great Britain stands ready to back up your efforts against France. Make use of the British offer while it stands.

Option 4 Take no action for the present.

France has done nothing to provoke a war. This entire crisis is only a scare conjured up by American fears about New Orleans. France did not close the port; that decision was made by a local Spanish official. The United States has been on reasonably good terms with the French, to whom it owes a debt of gratitude for its assistance in the war for independence.

Moreover, war is expensive in terms of both human life and dollars. Therefore, you should use war only as a last resort, and you certainly have not reached that stage yet. You have every reason to believe that you can live peacefully with France and its new North American possessions. Peace is far better than either defeat at the hands of the French or a forced alliance with Great Britain to prevent such a defeat.

Offers to buy New Orleans would not only be futile but could also cause political problems. Americans are still incensed over a recent attempt by French government officials to extort money from the United States in exchange for political favors. Americans could view an offer to purchase New Orleans as a bribe to induce France to leave the United States alone, and American pride will not allow for any such indignity.

YOU ARE THE PRESIDENT. WHAT IS YOUR DECISION?

Option 1 **Negotiate to buy New Orleans from the French.**

Option 2 **Attack the Spanish and seize New Orleans immediately.**

Option 3 **Declare war on France.**

Option 4 **Take no action for the present.**

President Thomas Jefferson chose *Option 1*.

Jefferson believed that the United States would not survive very long unless it secured its western borders. He considered New Orleans crucial to American interests. In a private letter to French officials, he wrote that "the day that France takes possession of New Orleans, we must marry ourselves to the British fleet and nation, take over Spanish America, and eject France."

Yet Jefferson disliked the idea of "marrying" the United States to Great Britain, and he hated the thought of war with France. He believed that even purchasing land at a high price was cheaper than fighting a war over that land.

Given Napoleon's designs for a world empire, Jefferson admitted that he could not "count with confidence on obtaining New Orleans from France for money." But he wanted to try anyway. In January 1803, the president sent James Monroe across the Atlantic Ocean to help the American ambassador in France attempt to negotiate the purchase of New Orleans.

To ease tensions and smooth the way for possible negotiations, Jefferson took the official position that Juan Morales had acted on his own in closing New Orleans to Americans, and that neither France nor Spain had ordered the move.

President Thomas Jefferson (1743-1826) had to decide what sacrifices were necessary to secure New Orleans for the United States.

Thirteen years after negotiating an agreement with France for New Orleans, James Monroe (1758-1831) was elected the fifth president of the United States.

RESULT

Jefferson benefited from an enormous streak of good fortune. France's first steps in establishing its New World empire ended in disaster. A bitterly cold winter froze the French fleet in a Dutch harbor and prevented it from sailing to New Orleans. All Napoleon's hopes then rested with the expedition he had sent to the Caribbean island of Santo Domingo to put down a rebellion led by former slaves. After reestablishing French control of this base of operations, the army was to proceed to the North American continent.

An outbreak of yellow fever, however, brought Napoleon's dreams of conquest to a halt. The disease, together with attacks by the rebels, decimated the French expedition in a matter of weeks. The few survivors among the 30,000 soldiers who had sailed to Santo Domingo returned to France without having secured the island.

The loss of so many well-trained troops in a futile effort crushed Napoleon. He couldn't stand to think of his powerful army struck down and defeated by disease. At that point, he abandoned his plan of a New World empire and concentrated instead on the more familiar arena of Europe.

To help finance his European conquests, Napoleon decided to sell off French possessions in North America. "I renounce Louisiana," he told his aides. "It is not only New Orleans I cede, it is the whole colony, without reserve." French and U.S. negotiators quickly settled on a price. On May 2, 1803, they signed an agreement that gave the United States the entire Louisiana Territory, stretching from New Orleans to what is now the state of Montana, in exchange for $15 million. The Louisiana Purchase added more than 827,000 square miles of land to the United States, nearly doubling the size of the young nation.

The U.S. flag replaces the flag of France in New Orleans after the United States purchased the Louisiana Territory in 1803.

Jefferson's purchase of the Louisiana Territory probably owed more to luck than to design. One historian says that, given the prevailing opinion of Napoleon's ambitions, had the French not been hit by disasters, Jefferson had "about as much chance of buying New Orleans as he did Paris."

Had these negotiations failed, as even Jefferson expected, war was a distinct possibility. In that case, the president could have been accused of squandering his advantage while he dallied over his purchase offer.

Even though Jefferson succeeded in making a deal with France, the rival Federalist party criticized his efforts. Massachusetts congressman George Cabot sneered at Jefferson for paying money to gain something that France was helpless to protect. The sale, according to Cabot,

Massachusetts congressman George Cabot (1752-1823) believed that President Jefferson paid far too much money for the Louisiana Territory.

favored France in every way. France rid itself "of an encumbrance that wounded her pride," received money, and regained "the friendship of our populace." The Federalists claimed that if Jefferson had seized New Orleans before negotiating, he could have bought Louisiana for a much lower price.

The American people, however, overwhelmingly approved the president's actions. Following the purchase, Jefferson's popularity soared, and the Federalists' fortunes fell. Most historians agree that Jefferson pulled off the real-estate deal of the century. For a relatively low price, he secured the mouth of the Mississippi River and nearly doubled the size of the nation. He managed this without either firing a shot or falling into an unwanted alliance with Great Britain.

Looking back on events, the president was thankful he had not "seized New Orleans as our Federalist maniacs wished." He proudly observed, "By a reasonable and peaceable process, we have obtained in four months what would have cost us seven years of war, 100,000 human lives, and $100 million."

2

SAFETY AT SEA
June 1812

The titanic struggle between the European powers of Great Britain and France has caught America's fledgling shipping industry in its crossfire. The British have imposed a naval blockade against their French enemy. They reserve the right to enforce this blockade by searching neutral vessels and taxing goods headed for Europe. Since 1805, British policy has been to seize any vessel attempting to trade with France or its allies.

France has countered by declaring its intention to seize any ship that submits to these British rules. Thus, American ships cannot sail in European waters without offending one of these two nations. Both British and French warships have captured dozens of American ships, seized their goods, and even imprisoned their crews.

To give the warring parties incentive to respect American rights, Congress has said that if either side ends its quarantine against American shipping, the U.S. government will give the other country a short time to follow suit. If it does not, the United States will then stop trading with that country.

France says it will repeal its quarantine. So far, however, you have seen little evidence of a repeal: The French continue to hold American ships, sailors, and goods. Britain does not believe France really intends to abandon its blockade. The British, too, have given no indication that they intend to ease their quarantine.

Americans are tired of yielding to the outrages of the European powers and are urging you to take action.

BACKGROUND

Of the two adversaries, France presents the greater threat to world peace. French emperor Napoleon Bonaparte has demonstrated the ambition and the ability to conquer all of Europe.

British foreign policy has one primary objective: defeat Napoleon. For years, the British have lived in fear that the French, who boast the most powerful army in the world, would invade and conquer Britain. The British believe their navy represents the world's only protection from the man whom they view as the most dangerous tyrant the modern world has ever known. They believe that other nations should at least support their efforts to stop Napoleon's world conquest.

Napoleon Bonaparte, one of the most powerful leaders in world history, earned the nickname "Little Colonel" while attending military school as a teenager.

As part of their plan to thwart France, the British have tried to cut France's source of supplies from the outside world. That includes not only military supplies but many commercial supplies as well. Although this hurts American shipping, the British argue that Americans must put up with the inconvenience for the good of the free world.

Yet Britain's policy of impressment humiliates and infuriates Americans far more than anything Napoleon has done. Impressment, the practice of stopping American ships and forcing American sailors to serve in the British navy, happens because harsh conditions aboard British ships cause many of their crew members to desert. Although British warships have established their dominance over the French navy in the Atlantic Ocean, the British are far from overconfident. They desperately need sailors to operate their vessels and to keep Napoleon at bay.

Many of the British deserters have fled to American ports. There they have applied for U.S. citizenship and then signed on aboard American ships. The British claim the right to recover these deserters. By maintaining that anyone born a British subject remains one for life and is therefore eligible for impressment into the British navy when duty demands, the British have shown a disdain for U.S. independence.

The British navy has already impressed as many as 6,000 U.S. citizens. This infuriating practice has led to dangerous incidents at sea. Last year, when British ships lurked off the coast of New York to impress American seamen, the United States sent the USS *President* warship to defend American shipping rights. The *President* attacked a British ship, killing 9 people on board and wounding 23 more.

Britain has recently poured fuel on the fire with the insulting proposal that all American ships must apply for British trade licenses before they can sail to the continent of Europe. Many Americans living in the western

Sending the USS President *to attack British ships was one of the first steps the United States took to stop Britain from capturing American sailors.*

states also accuse the British of encouraging Indians to attack American settlements.

Following the course laid by the founders of the United States who warned against getting involved in European affairs, America has avoided allying itself with either France or Britain. However, even if the government were inclined to seek an alliance with one of these great powers, American sympathies have never clearly favored one side over the other. Because of their British heritage, many Americans lean toward Britain. Others harbor resentment toward Britain for its treatment of its former colonies and have not forgotten that France supported the United States during the American Revolutionary War.

The United States rarely lives up to its name. Rather than acting as a united force, it often operates as a loose organization of states, each looking after its own interests. It has no standing national army and relies entirely on state militia (temporary soldiers summoned in time of emergency) for defense. Its navy is too small to pose a serious challenge to either the British or the French navies.

THE DECISION IS YOURS.

How will you get European powers to respect America's claims of neutrality on the sea?

Option 1 Stand up to both Britain and France. Declare war on both if necessary.

Nobody wants war, but the arrogance of the European powers has exceeded the bounds of reason. America's honor and self-respect is at stake. As the Virginia legislature has declared, "However highly we value the blessings of peace, and however we may deprecate the evils of war, the period has now arrived when peace, as we now have it, is disgraceful, and war is honorable." Former president Thomas Jefferson, who twisted himself into knots trying to avoid war with either power during his term, now says "war or abject submission are the only alternatives left to us."

"Light-horse" Harry Lee, a respected commander during the American Revolution, argues that the United States is already at war with these countries. Lee urges Americans to fight back. "A continuance in the present state of half war is . . . debasing to the nation and nearly as injurious as war itself to individual prosperity," he says. "It is better to fight our way to future peace, than to drag on in this state of disputation and irritation."

While Britain appears to be the greater offender, France has also done its share of provoking. The French claim they are now honoring American neutrality, but evidence is slow in coming. American congressional leader Henry Clay says, "[If there are] no accounts of justice having been done by France to the United States, and if no money being paid or promised" for the damages already done by French ships, then war should be declared on them as well.

The United States cannot hope to match the military power of these two giants. But since Britain and France are too busy fighting each other to be greatly concerned with the United States, now would be a good time to assert your rights.

Henry Clay (1777-1852), a U.S. senator and leader of the "war hawks," stirred up enthusiasm within the Senate for the idea of going to war against Britain.

Option 2 **Declare war on Britain alone.**

The United States must stand up for its rights as a free nation. But the idea of the small, militarily weak United States battling the two strongest powers in the world at the same time is sheer lunacy. The best strategy for the United States is to play the European powers against each other.

Although you have ample cause for declaring war against either Britain or France, Britain has been the worse offender. As Thomas Jefferson says, "We resist the enterprises of Britain first, because they first come vitally home to us." France at least shows some promise of easing its restrictions on your shipping. Britain's continued disdain for your shipping concerns, together with its impressment policy and trouble-making among the native Indians on your frontiers, makes them your first target.

Furthermore, Britain's attitude signals that it might not be completely willing to concede your independence. British policies appear to be designed to keep America in submission to British rule—making it little more than a colony.

Finally, the British are vulnerable to American military attacks. Their territory of Canada just to the north of the United States is sparsely populated and poorly defended. The United States could win a quick victory there. This would then put you in a good bargaining position for gaining concessions from Britain. France, on the other hand, has no such tempting targets in North America.

Option 3 **Impose economic sanctions on Britain.**

Wars are expensive and tragic. American political sage Benjamin Franklin had said there has never been a good war or a bad peace. Americans hold themselves to be above the mindless war mentality that has ravaged Europe for centuries. Why stoop to the self-destructive habit of war? Instead, why not show Europe that armed conflict is not the only way to solve problems?

A far more civilized way of changing Britain's mind is to impose economic sanctions. Make the British see that their economic interests are not well served by treating the United States with disdain.

The United States is one of Britain's best trading customers. If you suspend all trade between the two countries, British commerce will suffer. When British merchants feel the pinch, they will put pressure on their government to deal fairly with the United States.

This policy will influence the British government without risking American lives and prestige in war. By limiting British imports, you may also give a boost to American industries that will then be called upon to meet the demand for products that formerly came from Britain.

Americans continue to heed the advice of Benjamin Franklin (1706-1790), inventor, postmaster general, and Revolutionary War diplomat to France.

Option 4 Take no action at this time.

No country should go to war without the overwhelming support for that action by its people. A strong minority in the United States, led by the Federalist party, opposes war with Britain.

While some Federalists concede that the United States would be justified in declaring war, they warn that a declaration of war would be "the death warrant of the country's prosperity." Virginia congressman Daniel Sheffey argues, "I must be persuaded that there is a national hope that war will remedy the evil which we experience." The Federalists, who are particularly strong in the New England states, do not see that war will accomplish anything. They point out that the United States only recently fought for eight difficult years to gain their independence.

Why should we now invite another war with Britain and give the British another chance to gain back their former colonies? Americans are woefully unprepared for war. They have rejected the idea of a permanent national army. They prefer to rely on hastily organized state militia, and then only for defense. Many balk at taking the offensive and crossing the border into Canada, even if American commanders argue that this strategy is needed to win the war. Americans are also firm in their dislike of taxes, which would be necessary to finance a war.

As for economic sanctions, the government tried that route in 1807, and it failed miserably. In December that year, at President Jefferson's request, Congress passed the Embargo Act against British shipping. This act nearly caused the ruin of the American shipping industry and imposed severe hardships on American farmers, who no longer had a foreign market for their goods. American merchants complained that the Embargo Act was "rapidly teaching [the British] to do without us."

Citizens in the New England states, who depended on commerce with Britain for their livelihood, openly defied the Embargo Act. Also, the federal government depended on import tariffs as its main source of income. By barring British commerce from American ports, the government cut off the funds it needed to operate. Even Jefferson made no objection when Congress repealed the Embargo Act in 1809.

The present crisis is primarily a result of the war between France and Britain. Both countries have imposed emergency measures that they will surely disband when the war ends. The best thing to do is to resist the hotheads who are demanding war. If you show patience, the war will end, and these problems will solve themselves without risk.

YOU ARE THE PRESIDENT.
WHAT IS YOUR DECISION?

Option 1 **Stand up to both Britain and France. Declare war on both if necessary.**

Option 2 **Declare war on Britain alone.**

Option 3 **Impose economic sanctions on Britain.**

Option 4 **Take no action at this time.**

President James Madison (1751-1836), a student of history, relied on his knowledge of the past when deciding how to respond to Britain's policy of capturing U.S. citizens.

President James Madison chose *Option 2*.

Madison detested warfare. His studies of history had taught him that wars create disastrous public debts and that warring governments tend to assume emergency powers that restrict the liberty of the people. He cited "national degradation as the only calamity which is greater than war."

While Madison admitted that both Britain and France had committed hostile acts against the United States, he considered Britain's conduct the greater insult to the integrity of the United States. He believed that the U.S. government had exhausted every peaceful means of dealing with Britain. For him, the only question that remained was whether Britain's acts constituted a "national degradation" that called for war.

Madison believed that government officials should take heed of public opinion. Because he sensed that a majority of the citizens favored war with Britain, that was the course he advised. On June 1, 1812, Madison sent a war message to Congress. He listed the following as reasons for war: 1) Britain's impressment of American citizens, harassment of American shores, and illegal blockades against American shipping, and 2) Britain's encouragement of Indian hostilities on the western frontier.

RESULT

President Madison's recommendation received a lukewarm endorsement by Congress, which declared war on Britain by a vote of 79-49 in the House of Representatives and only 19-13 in the Senate. New England strongly opposed what it called "Mr. Madison's War" and talked about separating from the United States. The Massachusetts legislature went so far as to pass a resolution encouraging citizens to impede the war effort.

The War of 1812 nearly destroyed the United States. Incompetent American generals botched the invasion of Canada. Despite spectacular victories by American warships in the Atlantic Ocean early into the war, Britain's powerful navy easily gained control of the U.S. coastline.

Worse yet, Britain soon defeated Napoleon and so was able to concentrate its entire military might against the United States. In 1814, British troops scattered a ragged American militia outside Washington, D.C., and then burned the U.S. Capitol to the ground. At that point, the United States was on the verge of utter defeat—its government bankrupt and its coasts defenseless against attack.

All other political issues took a back seat as Americans fought for their survival. The Americans' courageous defense of Baltimore, which inspired Francis Scott Key to write the "Star-Spangled Banner," dashed British prospects for a decisive victory. Then, while the two sides were arranging a peace treaty, American troops under Andrew Jackson annihilated a large British army at New Orleans.

In 31 months of fighting, the United States accomplished very little. The nation gained no significant concessions from Britain, yet lost no territory.

Composer and poet Francis Scott Key (1779-1843) served as the U.S. attorney for the District of Columbia from 1833 to 1841.

General Andrew Jackson received national acclaim after leading the United States to a decisive victory against the British in New Orleans.

HINDSIGHT

The War of 1812 may well have been unnecessary. Under pressure from merchants who were feeling the economic pinch from strained British-American commerce, the British government removed many restrictions on American shipping before the U.S. Congress had formally declared war. Slow transatlantic communications, however, prevented the news from reaching the United States in time to avoid the war. Although issues such as impressment remained as obstacles to peace, the British concessions might have opened the way to a deal between the two countries had the Americans waited a few more weeks more before taking action.

Britain's defeat of France also made Britain's vigorous pursuit of impressment unnecessary. Had the United States been more patient, this issue, too, might have faded away. Some historians argue that Britain's shift in position in response to its merchants indicates that economic sanctions may have worked, although others point to the failure of the Embargo Act as evidence that sanctions would have done more harm than good.

Against these events, waging one of the most unpopular wars in American history seemed a needless and even reckless risk. The war nearly split New England from the rest of the country and came perilously close to squandering the independence so painfully gained from Britain during the Revolutionary War.

On the other hand, historian Robert Rutland has argued that, given the mood of the country at the time, "If he had tried any other course, Madison would have been a discredited president and might have been impeached."

Fortunately for Madison and the United States, the president's decision turned out well. When the War of 1812 turned into a war of survival, most Americans buried their differences and united in a common cause. They greeted the victories in Baltimore and New Orleans with both relief and a new sense of pride in their country. The United States had stood up for its rights as an independent nation against a world power and held its ground. As Albert Gallatin, one of Madison's advisers, wrote, the war made Americans "feel and act more as a nation; and I hope the permanency of the Union is thereby better secured."

The American people provided Madison with the most satisfying vindication of his decision. Voters overwhelmingly rejected the Federalists who had opposed the war, and the party quickly faded into obscurity. Perhaps the most satisfying support of Madison's policy came from Boston. A group of that city's citizens sent Madison a message apologizing for the behavior of their region during the conflict and thanked him for his efforts.

3

INDIAN POLICY
1832

The cultural friction between white settlers and Indian tribes has often sparked outbursts of violence on the North American frontiers. After roughly three centuries of contact between these groups, the United States has come nowhere near a peaceful solution to this conflict.

In recent years, relations between the Cherokees and citizens of the southeastern United States have reached a critical point. The Cherokees have organized themselves into an Indian nation within the boundaries of the United States. They want whites to respect their legal claim to the land and their right to govern themselves according to their own laws.

But Georgians are opposed to what they view as a hostile foreign people setting up their own government within Georgia's sovereign boundaries. They want the Indians removed, and they maintain that the federal government is obligated to do just that.

Both sides insist that the federal government must honor its promises to them. Unfortunately, the United States has entered into two separate contradictory agreements. It has signed treaties with the Cherokees that recognize Cherokee ownership of a large area of land covering parts of Georgia, Alabama, Tennessee, and North Carolina. But in March 1802, Georgia ceded its western lands to the federal government for $1,250,000 on the condition that the government would move the Cherokees living on the land that Georgia claimed.

You cannot keep one promise without breaking the other. Yet conflict between the two sides is growing so intense that you must take some action.

BACKGROUND

The Cherokee nation numbers approximately 20,000 individuals. They have made a great effort to adapt their society to the ways of the whites. The Cherokees have developed a written language, a constitution, and their own newspaper. They have compiled documentation of their wealth, adopted the U.S. practice of owning black slaves, and gained familiarity with the U.S. legal system. Although their past relations with U.S. settlers have been hostile at times, the Cherokees have been an ally to the whites in recent decades. Less than 20 years ago, they helped U.S. soldiers in their battles against the Creek Indians.

Georgia, however, has been waiting impatiently for the federal government to remove the Cherokees and to open Cherokee lands to white settlers. The discovery of gold on Cherokee land in 1828 only fueled the state's determination to gain control of these lands. Frustrated by the federal government's failure to act, the state began taking matters into its own hands. In 1829, the Georgia legislature passed an act that incorporated a large area of the Cherokee nation into state counties and made the Indians living there subject to state laws.

In an effort to pressure the Indians into moving out, the state legislature has passed laws that discriminate terribly against Indians. For example, one law states that "no Indian or descendant of Indians residing within the . . . Cherokee nation of Indians shall be deemed a competent witness in any court of this state to which a white person may be a party." Because Cherokees are not allowed to testify against whites in U.S. courts, whites can harass, assault, and steal from the Cherokees without threat of punishment.

The Cherokees also are incensed because Georgia has declared all gold mines on Indian lands to be the property of the state and is setting up a lottery to distribute Indian land to state citizens.

The Cherokee national council has forbidden individual members of the nation to yield to the pressures to move west. The council has threatened death to those Cherokees who negotiate to sell their lands, and Cherokees have burned the homes of whites attempting to build on Cherokee land.

Georgia's inhumane stand and the Cherokees' refusal to be intimidated have created the potential for a bloodbath. The Georgia state guard stands ready to attack at the slightest provocation. If war breaks out, the outnumbered and outgunned Cherokees have little chance of surviving.

THE DECISION IS YOURS.

How do you calm the tensions to avoid violence between the Cherokees and the whites?

Option 1 Expel the Cherokees from Georgia.

You cannot honor both promises. Since you have to come down on one side or the other, you have no choice but to act in favor of the U.S. citizens. Indians just do not mix well with those of European backgrounds. They are too intent on preserving their ways to live peacefully side by side with white settlements.

From a practical standpoint, you have no choice but to clear the Indians out. American settlers, who are continually moving and settling into the woodlands around Indians lands, have little patience with Indian ways. Determined to get rid of the Indians, the overwhelming majority of these settlers is so rabidly anti-Indian that if you do not move the Indians out of their way, the settlers will do so themselves.

In addition, the federal government cannot interfere with the power of the states to enforce their own laws, even those that are shockingly unfair to Indians. The laws that Georgia has enacted are just a preview of what is in store for the Indians if you do not move them out of harm's way. The only permanent solution to violence between Indians and whites is to to get the Indians away from the populated areas of the United States.

Option 2 **Put pressure on the Cherokees to sell their lands in exchange for new lands west of the Mississippi.**

The attitudes of the Georgians and the Cherokees have put you in an impossible situation. You cannot ignore the federal government's promise to Georgia. If you do, the Georgia guard will act on its own to expel the Indians and will not be gentle about it. Yet a lawful government cannot simply evict the Indians from lands that they legally own.

The best solution is to persuade the Cherokees that moving west is in their best interest. The Cherokees are well aware of Georgia's contempt for Indians, and they know that the state will go to great lengths to make them miserable. Georgia is not unique in this respect. Many white settlers all along the North American frontier hate Indians and would lose no sleep if all of the Indians were killed.

Obviously, these are not the kind of people the Cherokees want for neighbors. If the Cherokees stay where they are, the Georgians will cheat, rob, abuse, and assault them until they are goaded into violence. Even if they act in self-defense, the white settlers will react by destroying the Cherokee nation.

Although the Cherokees would be giving up their traditional lands, you can help ease their loss. Your federal government can pay them for their land, then provide them with new lands west of the Mississippi.

Option 3 **Send federal troops to protect the Indians' rights.**

While most U.S. citizens look to their own interests and have little concern for the problems of Indians, Georgia has overstepped the bounds of decency. Its oppressive tactics against the Cherokees have outraged a large segment of the population. As one reporter wrote, the whites have committed "brutalities sufficient to fire the blood and arouse the indignation of every American." This treatment is especially unjust in view of the aid the Cherokees provided to the U.S. government during the Creek War.

Furthermore, earlier this year the Supreme Court ruled that Georgia's laws concerning the Cherokee are unconstitutional. Writing for the Court in the case of *Worcester v. Georgia*, Chief Justice John Marshall ruled that these laws violated a solemn treaty between the United States and the Cherokees. "The Cherokee nation," wrote Marshall, "is a distinct community, occupying its own territory, with boundaries accurately described, in which the laws of Georgia have no right to enter but with the assent of the Cherokees themselves or in conformity with treaties and the acts of Congress."

This ruling declares that Georgia is in the wrong in this dispute. Therefore, you have no right to pressure or force the Cherokees into moving. You must come down on the side of the Indians.

John Marshall (1755-1835), chief justice of the U.S. Supreme Court from 1801 to 1835, believed that the Cherokees had every right to remain on their own land in Georgia.

Georgia has chosen to ignore the Supreme Court ruling. By doing so, it defies the power of the federal government, which you are sworn to uphold. Georgia has left you with no choice but to send in federal troops to enforce the court's decision and protect the rights of the Cherokees.

Option 4 **Negotiate with Georgia and seek accommodation between that state and the Cherokees.**

While you have a moral and legal obligation to consider the rights of the Indians, you must realize the impracticality of protecting the Indians with federal troops. The Cherokees control approximately 7 million acres of land, much of it wilderness. The United States would need to patrol the entire border of the Cherokee nation against intruders. The United States, however, has only a small number of soldiers in uniform—certainly not enough to provide adequate protection for the Indians.

You must realize that Georgians, as well as settlers in the surrounding states, are unshakable in their determination to expel the Indians. A few federal soldiers will not intimidate the whites into giving up their cause. By sending troops to protect the Indians, you will not only infuriate the states but will probably trigger more violence than ever, including the possibility of a civil war.

Instead, you should remedy the mistake the federal government made in 1802 when it promised something to Georgia that it could not legally deliver. The federal government could end the dispute between Georgia and the Cherokees by purchasing Georgia's claims to Indian territory.

This could prove expensive, though. Georgia would demand a high price in exchange for its claims, especially since gold has been discovered on Cherokee land. But in the long run, this option would more than pay for itself. Granting compensation to Georgia could defuse emotions and eliminate the expense of providing federal troops to protect Indian rights. It would also eliminate the expense of moving the Cherokees.

Having the federal government take over dealings with the Indians would give you the opportunity to work out solutions to Indian problems in an atmosphere free from bitterness. You could set up programs to help the Indian and white communities understand each other better. This type of program would be particularly effective with the Cherokees, who have shown an exceptional ability to adapt to white society.

YOU ARE THE PRESIDENT.
WHAT IS YOUR DECISION?

Option 1   **Expel the Cherokees from Georgia.**

Option 2   **Put pressure on the Cherokees to sell their lands in exchange for new lands west of the Mississippi.**

Option 3   **Send federal troops to protect the Indians' rights.**

Option 4   **Negotiate with Georgia and seek accommodation between that state and the Cherokees.**

Andrew Jackson (1767-1845), often called the first "common man" to become president, had years of military and legal experience behind him when he was faced with deciding how to handle the Cherokees in Georgia.

President Andrew Jackson chose *Option 2*.

The racial prejudice of his times shaped Jackson's policy toward the Indians. According to Jackson, "All preceding experiments for the improvement of the Indian have failed. It seems now an established fact that they cannot live in contact with a civilized community and prosper." He blamed the situation on the Indians, claiming they had "neither the intelligence, the industry, the moral habits, nor the desire of improvement to allow them to remain among U.S. citizens," he stated.

The president saw no point in wasting federal troops in a futile effort to prevent the inevitable conflict between neighboring Indians and whites. Responding to Indian complaints about Georgia, Jackson answered, "I cannot interfere with the laws of that state to protect you."

When Chief Justice Marshall, in the *Worcester* Supreme Court decision, told Jackson that he not only could but should interfere with Georgia's unconstitutional laws, Jackson simply ignored the Court. Some sources report him as saying, "John Marshall has made his decision; let him enforce it now if he can."

Having determined that Indian and white communities could not live together in peace and that he could not protect the Cherokees, Jackson decided to move the Indians. Despite his lack of respect for Indian culture, the president sympathized with the Cherokee, with whom he had fought in the Creek War.

Part of his reason for moving the Indians was that he feared for their safety if they stayed where they were.

He described himself as a humanitarian charged with the responsibility of saving the Indians from extermination.

Jackson, therefore, did not simply ignore past treaties and shove the Cherokees off their land. He instead tried to persuade the Indians to sell their property for new land in the unpopulated west, where he could better guarantee their safety. He decided on a policy of paying the Indians for their land and providing funds for their removal.

RESULT

While negotiations took place between federal officials and Cherokee leaders, white settlers continued to encroach on Indian territory. Surveyors overran the land, and whites assaulted Indians. In 1835, the Georgia state guard shut down the Cherokee press.

Later that year, Andrew Jackson's agents eventually negotiated a treaty with a group representing the Cherokees. The Cherokees agreed to sell their eastern lands for a net price of $3 million ($9 million, minus the $6 million the federal government charged them for the move). The treaty gave the Cherokee two years to leave their homes.

Jackson praised the agreement, saying that by arranging the peaceful removal of the Indians, "we have accomplished something monumental and everlasting." Even the Whigs, the political party opposed to Jackson, described the treaty terms given to the Cherokees as "exceedingly liberal to say the least."

However, what Jackson referred to as his "successful experiment" quickly proved to be an illusion. Fewer than 100 Cherokees had been present at the meeting in which the treaty was approved. They were hardly representative of their people, who overwhelmingly rejected the treaty. Cherokee leader John Ross compiled the signatures of 14,000 Cherokees who opposed selling their lands.

When the two-year grace period ended in 1837, by which time Jackson had left office, most Cherokees refused to leave their homes. In 1837 and 1838, federal and state troops then rounded them up and herded them into prison camps. The departing Cherokees saw their homes burned by a mob of whites that followed the soldiers.

So began the tragic event known among the Cherokees as the "Trail of Tears." Treating them like animals, whites boxed up the Cherokees the into railroad cars for the first leg of their 800-mile journey to Oklahoma, then forced them to walk the final leg. The Indians were treated so harshly that of 18,000 Cherokees who started the trek, approximately 4,000 died before they reached their destination in Oklahoma.

Many years later, a veteran soldier was moved to write, "I fought through the Civil War and have seen men shot to pieces and slaughtered by the thousands, but the Cherokee removal was the cruelest I ever saw. "

Retired from the presidency and unable to change the circumstances, Andrew Jackson anguished over the plight of the Indians. He did not expect the removal to take place under such brutal conditions. He truly believed the Indians would be safer if they left Georgia. Considering the prevailing attitudes of the whites who were encroaching on the Cherokee nation and the restrictive laws of Georgia, that may have been the case.

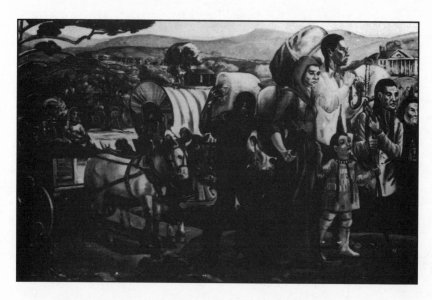

This 1939 "Trail of Tears" mural by Elizabeth Janes illustrates the relocation of the Cherokees from Georgia to Oklahoma during the 1830s.

Cherokee leader John Ross (1790-1866), who had tried to prevent the Indian removal from Georgia, served under General Andrew Jackson during the War of 1812.

But Jackson's stubbornness and lack of respect for Indian culture had closed his mind to other options and set the stage for one of the most tragic and shameful episodes in the nation's history. Although the Trail of Tears took place after Jackson's term of office, he bears responsibility for the event.

The Jackson administration was so eager to accomplish removal that it refused to back the nation's highest court against Georgia's repressive laws. Jackson violated principles of fairness by maneuvering to get a few Cherokees to sign a treaty that the vast majority of them did not approve. The Jackson administration then used the treaty to break past federal promises to the Indians and to evict them under inhumane conditions.

4

OREGON TERRITORY
Spring 1846

Unsettled boundaries between nations stand as open invitations to conflict. The disputed ownership of the vast Oregon Territory along the northwest coast of the American continent has long been one of those crises waiting to happen. Based on the travels of their explorers in this region, both the United States and Great Britain claim the entire Oregon Territory from California to Alaska.

Neither side, however, has pressed the issue too hard. Following the War of 1812, the two nations formed a commission to settle the boundary. When this commission could not produce a compromise acceptable to both sides, Great Britain and the United States found a unique solution to their conflicting claims. In a treaty signed on October 20, 1818, the two nations agreed to "joint occupation." This treaty granted both countries equal rights of passage and use in this wilderness area. Each nation was free to terminate the agreement whenever it wished. At that time, the two would work out a more conventional and permanent settlement of their claims.

This friendly arrangement worked out well enough at first, when Oregon was little more than a shared trapping ground for fur traders. But American settlers have recently begun to move into the area. As their population grows, these people are eager to set up a more organized government under the U.S. flag.

The previous U.S. administration began negotiations with Great Britain for permanent boundaries in Oregon. The talks have so far been unsuccessful. Meanwhile, arguments are flying at you from both sides. American settlers have petitioned Congress to accept Oregon as an American territory. A vocal group of American political leaders supports them and insists that all of Oregon belongs to the United States. Others fear that any American demands over Oregon will lead to a disastrous war with Great Britain.

BACKGROUND

There are three logical points of division in Oregon: 1) If the U.S. claims all of Oregon, the northern boundary of this region will reach the latitude of 54° 40′. The Alaskan land north of that line belongs to Russia. 2) If the U.S. claims land only as far as the northern boundaries of American territory to the east of Oregon, the boundary will fall to the 49th parallel. 3) If the U.S. claims only the land actually settled by Americans, the boundary will follow the Columbia River, which winds south of the 49th parallel.

Between 1842 and 1845, the number of U.S. citizens living in Oregon grew from 400 to more than 5,000. Most of them lived south of the Columbia River, along with 900 British and Canadians. Roughly 900 more British and Canadians with ties to Great Britain's fur-trapping Hudson's Bay Company lived north of the Columbia. Recently, a large wagon train arrived that more than doubled the American population in Oregon, and more Americans are on their way to Oregon this year. Some of these people are planning to settle north of the Columbia.

Great Britain is willing to set a boundary at the Columbia River. But the American people want to expand their borders as far as possible, and they have been steadily moving into their western territories in search of a better life. Many of these settlers claim that the United States is a special nation that should spread across the entire continent, advancing the cause of liberty and justice wherever it goes. This concept of "Manifest Destiny" is fueling the recent American decision to annex the republic of Texas and to wrestle California away from Mexico.

Recently, an active group of people has taken up the cry of "54, 40 or fight!" Insisting the United States owns all of Oregon, they are willing to go to war if Great Britain disputes this. They demonstrated their influence when American settlers in Oregon petitioned

Oregon settlers put their wagon on a "float boat" to travel down the Columbia River.

Congress to set up a territorial government. The House of Representatives responded by overwhelmingly passing legislation to organize a territorial government for all of Oregon. It even provided money for forts to back this government. The Senate declined to vote on the matter only because the administration assured them that it was on the verge of breakthrough in negotiations with Great Britain. That breakthrough never came.

Sentiment for 54° 40′ remains strong. In 1844, you won the presidency running on a campaign platform that claimed all of Oregon for the United States. Yet you did not win a majority of the popular vote and were elected only because your opposition was split into two factions. Some members of your own party are uncomfortable with its aggressive stance. Senator Hopkins Turney of Tennessee warns that a potential split over Oregon policy could wreck your party.

Great Britain is not a nation to trifle with. It is easily the dominant military power in the world—far stronger than the United States. The Hudson's Bay Company is determined to keep its possessions in Oregon and has great influence with its British government.

THE DECISION IS YOURS.

What policy will you pursue in Oregon?

Option 1 Insist on all of Oregon up to 54° 40´.

Your party adopted a platform promising the "reoccupation of Oregon" and made it an issue in the campaign. Because the American people accepted this platform and voted you into office, you must follow through on your promise.

Oregon is part of the North American continent; it lies nowhere near Great Britain. The people who are flocking to Oregon and who will continue to move there are U.S. citizens. Few British have arrived in the past decade, and few are expected in the near future. Government should exist only by the consent of the governed, and the majority of those likely to live in Oregon wants to be part of the United States, not the British Empire.

Despite their claims of ownership, the British have no right dabbling in North America. Former U.S. president James Monroe made that clear when he formulated the Monroe Doctrine in 1823. That doctrine, which Americans have supported ever since, says that people living in the Western Hemisphere will no longer tolerate interference from Europe. As Monroe put it, "American continents . . . are henceforth not to be considered as subjects for future colonization by any European powers."

Many American leaders have come out in favor of the United States' right to Oregon up to 54° 40′. Former presidents John Tyler and John Quincy Adams acknowledged this right. Current Secretary of State James Buchanan advises that the "54, 40 men are the true friends of the administration."

This policy will probably mean war. But the United States should not back down on its principles for fear of Great Britain. Thirty years ago, when the the United States was weaker than it is today, the nation fought off the British in the War of 1812. The sparse British population in Oregon and the immense distance of the territory from Great Britain give the Americans a military edge. Michigan representative John Chapman boasts that "Michigan alone would take Canada in 90 days" if war should come.

Option 2 Insist on a boundary at the 49th parallel.

Regardless of your campaign platform, you should not let the 54° 40′ hotheads goad you into a fight with Great Britain. The claim that the United States owns all of Oregon is ridiculous. If Americans really believed that, then why did they agree to joint occupation with Great Britain all these years? The U.S. claim is based on the Lewis and Clark expedition of 1804-1806, but the British have been exploring and occupying northern sections of Oregon since 1713.

There is no reason to risk a war with the British when a logical compromise is at hand. A border at the 49th parallel would balance the fact that the British occupy the greater part of Oregon against the growing American numbers in the region. The boundary makes sense because it simply extends the existing American boundary with Canada to the Pacific Ocean.

Americans have a sound strategic reason for refusing to accept any boundary farther south of that line. The

Assigned by President Thomas Jefferson to explore the newly acquired Louisiana Territory during the early 1800s, Meriwether Lewis and William Clark encountered many Native American tribes while traveling from the Mississippi River to the Pacific coast.

west coast of southern Oregon has no decent harbors for shipping. Only by putting the boundary up at the 49th parallel would the United States get the shipping access it needs.

The previous U.S. president, John Tyler, has already blazed this trail for you. While affirming American rights to 54° 40′, Tyler proposed this compromise to the British in 1843. He even bent the border at the Pacific edge to allow Great Britain to keep Vancouver Island. The British, however, rejected this proposal.

John Tyler (1790-1862), who served as president from 1841 to 1845, believed the Oregon Territory belonged to the United States.

Option 3 **Settle the boundary at the Columbia River.**

Even the 49th parallel claim is bold. A more logical boundary would run between the present settlements of Canadians and Americans. Until this past year, few Americans even thought about settling north of the Columbia River, which drops well below the 49th parallel as it flows westward to the Pacific Ocean. While the British and Canadian population north of the Columbia is sparse, it is there nonetheless. The United States has no right to claim these settlements for itself.

The British have responded to American complaints about the lack of a good seaport by promising the United States free use of all British ports that lie between the 49th parallel and the Columbia River.

A strong minority in your party does not want to cross the British in this matter for fear of war. Many British leaders are firm in demanding the Columbia River as the border. While the British are more inclined to peace than war, this kind of border dispute is the one thing that touches a nerve. As one British official commented, his country's policy is to stay out of foreign disputes, "but an attempt of one Nation to seize and to appropriate to itself territory which belongs to another Nation is a different matter."

Despite America's strategic advantages in Oregon, this would be a poor time for Americans to let their greed get them into a war with Great Britain. The United States has just committed itself to fighting a major war against Mexico. Risking two wars at once would be foolish, especially when one of these is against a nation as powerful as Great Britain.

Option 4 **Continue joint occupation.**

While this may sound like a cowardly way to avoid the issue altogether, there are compelling reasons for going this route.

Relations between Great Britain and the United States are generally good, and trade between the two nations has helped both to flourish. Moreover, the Oregon economy is more dependent on Great Britain than on the United States because most American settlers in the region buy from and sell products to the Hudson's Bay Company. They would have difficulty surviving if they were unable to do this.

The British know that your claim to a large part of Oregon currently rests on shaky ground. Confident that their claim is valid, they offered to take the dispute to impartial international arbitration, with both countries abiding by the arbiter's decision.

John C. Calhoun, a former U.S. secretary of state, urges you not to commit the "profound blunder" of risking a war against a friendly nation and trading partner merely to get more wilderness to which the United States may or may not be entitled. Calhoun suggests that a strategy of "masterly inactivity" will give the United States what it wants without risk. By that he means that the influx of American settlers into Oregon will strengthen the U.S. claim to Oregon. Within a decade, Americans will so dominate the population of Oregon that an international arbiter would have to agree that the area should be placed under U. S. control.

Although John C. Calhoun (1782-1850) strongly believed in fighting the British during the War of 1812, he thought battling them over the Oregon Territory would be a mistake.

YOU ARE THE PRESIDENT. WHAT IS YOUR DECISION?

Option 1   Insist on all of Oregon up to 54° 40´.

Option 2   Insist on a boundary at the 49th parallel.

Option 3   Settle the boundary at the Columbia River.

Option 4   Continue joint occupation.

James K. Polk (1795-1849) said that settling the dispute over Oregon's border was one of his main objectives as president.

President James K. Polk chose *Option 2*.

Polk firmly believed in American expansion, as evidenced by his aggressive policy against Mexico that brought California and Texas into the Union. In his inaugural address, the president came out firmly in support of the 54° 40′ boundary. "Our title to . . . Oregon is clear and unquestionable," he declared.

Polk may have been bluffing in an effort to force the British from claiming the Columbia River as the boundary. When asked about his stand on the Oregon issue, Polk replied, "The only way to treat John Bull [Great Britain] is to look him square in the face." On the other hand, Polk may simply have feared that the United States' commitment to fighting a war against Mexico left it in a poor position to risk a second war against the mighty British Empire.

Either way, the president determined that the best thing to do was to back off from the extreme claim and try for a boundary at the 49th parallel. Polk realized this decision would expose him to the wrath of those in his own party who believed he had committed himself to supporting their 54° 40′ stance. The president protected himself by continuing to back 54° 40′ publicly while his own treaty negotiators were conferring with the British for a boundary at the 49th parallel.

RESULT

On June 6, 1846, American and British negotiators reached a boundary agreement setting the border at the 49th parallel that was almost identical to the proposal President Tyler had submitted. President Polk reluctantly submitted this treaty to the Senate for its consideration, knowing full well it would pass. As predicted, the Senate approved the measure by a comfortable margin.

During the 1840s, thousands of American settlers followed the Oregon Trail from Independence, Missouri, to Oregon City (shown here during the mid-1840s).

Polk did not escape criticism from the 54° 40´ supporters of his party. The expansionists, who took the defeat bitterly, suspected Polk of being dishonest in his statements supporting their position. Senator William Allen of Ohio resigned as chairman of the Senate Foreign Relations Committee to protest the treaty. But the anger never boiled into open revolt in Polk's Democratic party, and the president suffered no significant damage from the expansionists.

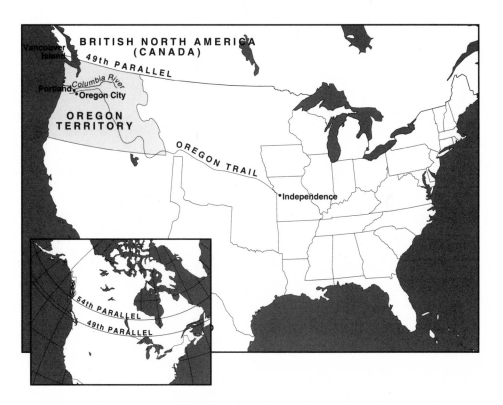

Acquiring the Oregon Territory in 1846 gave the United States the land now occupied by the states of Oregon, Washington, and a large part of Idaho.

The formation of an American Oregon Territory inspired hundreds of Americans to join those already setting off down the Oregon Trail in search of a new life.

HINDSIGHT

The aggressive attitude of Americans, particularly members of his own party living in the western states, left President Polk little room for negotiating with the British. But most historians agree that Polk made the most of the situation. In his hard-line statements on American rights and in his early negotiations, Polk skated along the edge of war with a dangerous military power. In backing off at just the right time, he succeeded where previous American negotiators had failed in getting the British to accept a compromise boundary.

This compromise added a large area of productive land—eventually the states of Oregon, Washington, and Idaho—without bloodshed and at no financial cost to the country. Historian Paul Bergeron concludes in his biography of the 11th president that "Polk brought about an amazing and bloodless conquest of territory."

5

SECESSION
February 1861

The United States has been locked in a tug-of-war over the issue of slavery. Northerners have outlawed slavery within their states and have sought to stop its spread into the western territories. Some of them have become increasingly vocal in demanding an end to what they consider to be an evil institution. Southerners, on the other hand, continue to honor the practice of slavery and have fought hard to extend its legality into the western territories.

Since the early years in the history of the nation, an uneasy balance of power between the two sections has held the country together. But in your final days as president, the dispute over slavery snapped the fragile threads that bound the Union. The election of Republican Abraham Lincoln, who opposes the spread of slavery

Whites often bought and sold black slaves at public auctions in the South.

into the territories, caused many Southerners to fear a loss of political power to the North. Angered by the prospect of interfering Northerners dictating how Southerners should live, South Carolina voted on December 20, 1860, to secede from the United States. In the past several weeks, Mississippi, Louisiana, Florida, Alabama, Georgia, and Texas have also dissolved their ties with the Union.

Most Northerners, as well as a strong minority of Southerners, insist that the act of secession is illegal according to the U.S. Constitution. Most Southerners, as well as a vocal minority of Northerners, believe states have the right to secede if they desire.

The presence of nine federal forts located in the seceding states further complicates this situation. These forts are the property of the United States government, and the seceding states are not likely to tolerate the presence of armed U.S. soldiers within their borders. Regardless of what actions you take concerning secession, you will either have to defend the forts or surrender them.

BACKGROUND

Only one other president has faced a similar crisis. In 1832, South Carolina reacted angrily to a federal law that slapped a high tariff on imported goods. Officials from South Carolina said they would not obey the law and insisted that states had the right to nullify or strike down any federal law with which they disagreed.

At that time, President Andrew Jackson had to decide whether to let South Carolina go its own way or to force it to comply with the law. Jackson embarked on a masterful campaign to get the state to withdraw its threat. Then, he rallied public opinion of the other states against South Carolina. Finally, he defused South Carolina's anger by asking Congress to reduce the tariff. Jackson's strategy worked. South Carolina abandoned its claim that a state had the right to nullify federal laws, and the nation avoided a civil war.

Your situation, however, is more difficult than what Jackson faced. Jackson had benefited by the strong support of Unionists in the South. Even the other southern states opposed South Carolina's radical doctrine of nullification. The present issue of slavery, however, has created a strong, united front in the Deep South. The seven seceding states will stand much more firmly against pressure or threats than South Carolina had done in 1832.

The heated passions of both sides have also left little room for compromise. Although the newly elected president says he is willing to leave slavery alone in the South, Southerners are insulted by the Northerners' attitude that slavery is wrong. They insist that the North back down on this point, but there is no chance that the North will do so.

The legal issues involved in this situation have never been settled. Your attorney general says that the Constitution authorizes you to call out the militia "whenever the laws of the United States shall be opposed by any state." But he asks you—and only you—to decide if the states that withdraw from the Union are bound by those laws.

THE DECISION IS YOURS.

What do you do about the southern states' secession from the Union?

Option 1 **Let the states secede and abandon federal forts in those states.**

A wide variety of advisers argue that the United States has no right to force a state to remain in the Union against its will. Horace Greeley, the influential editor of the *New York Tribune*, argues that the states have "a clear moral right to separate and form a nation." General Winfield Scott, commander-in-chief of the U.S. Army, takes the same view. He sees no point in embarking on a bloody civil war to force the South to stay in the Union.

Union general Winfield Scott (1786-1866) believed that the federal government should let the South leave the Union.

Pennsylvania judge George Woodward adds that southern secession is the fault of the North's meddling policies. "Let them go in peace. . . . We are the wrong doers. We have driven them off."

The federal forts in the South, meanwhile, are disasters waiting to happen. By trying to hold on to them, you would be angering the southern states and providing a convenient excuse for them to fight. At any rate, you cannot properly defend these forts. The United States has only 16,000 soldiers in its army, most of whom are stationed in the West. General Scott estimates you have only 400 troops to defend your nine forts. Any attempt to bring in reinforcements from the West will surely provoke the South to war.

There is still strong support among many Southerners for remaining in the Union. Your best course would be to ensure peace by abandoning the forts or, perhaps, by selling them to the South. If left alone, the southern states will eventually recognize they were wrong to secede and will rejoin the Union.

Option 2 Send an army to bring the seceding states back into the Union.

According to the Constitution, secession is illegal. Ironically, the strongest historical support for this position comes from a Southerner, former President Andrew Jackson. According to Jackson, because the states formed "a government, not a league," they do not possess any right to secede just because they do not agree with the will of the majority in the country. As a president sworn to defend the Constitution, you have no choice but to take action against those states that have seceded.

You cannot give in to the fear that you might be responsible for starting a war. That choice lies with the seceding states, not you. They can choose to disobey the laws, but your job is to enforce the law. According to Andrew Jackson, "disunion by armed force is treason." That means that if the South takes up arms to resist your efforts to regain control of the seceding states, then they are traitors whom you need to bring to justice.

Andrew Jackson was not afraid to use force to keep states in the Union. Although he did not actually send troops to subdue South Carolina, he clearly demonstrated that he would do so if that state did not back down. On his deathbed, Jackson regretted not having taken more decisive action in 1832. The former president insisted that, if he had it to do over again, he would have executed South Carolina political leader John C. Calhoun. "My country would have sustained me in the act, and his fate would have been a warning to traitors in all time to come," Jackson said.

While you do not have to go quite so far, you need to take the kind of firm action Jackson had shown to defuse the crisis.

Option 3 Allow the states to secede but hold on to the forts.

Some of your advisers agree that, according to the U.S. Constitution, secession is illegal. But they do not believe you should send troops against the seceding states because such military action would give those states a moral and legal right to leave the Union permanently. To support their stand, they quote former president James Madison, who said, "The use of force against a state . . . would probably be considered by the party attacked as a dissolution of all previous contracts by which it might be bound." Your advisers insist that this calls for gentler persuasion.

Since secession is illegal, however, you cannot just give in to the secessionists' every demand. These outlaw states have no right to take or interfere with federal property such as the forts. While confusion reigns as to whether a seceding state is part of the United States, the forts clearly belong to the federal government. If you refuse to defend this federal property, you will violate your oath to protect and defend the United States. Such timid behavior may also raise a storm of protest in the North that will make compromise between North and South impossible.

Defending the forts will give you an added political advantage. While many Americans don't like the idea of declaring war against the citizens of seceding states, they are intensely loyal to the United States. Should events lead you to consider war in this crisis, you will more easily win public support if the southern states begin the hostilities. An attack on the forts will put the South in the wrong. Many otherwise-reluctant Americans will leap to the defense of a flag that is under attack.

Option 4 **Organize a national convention to find a compromise solution.**

Given the emotions and disagreement over principles, this option will not be easy to implement. But you are in danger of becoming either the president who let the Union be destroyed or the president who started a terrible civil war. Neither alternative is appealing. You must do everything in your power to get the two sides together to promote understanding and compromise.

Despite the gloomy scenario, you still have reason to hope. Many Southerners do not understand that the newly elected Republicans have no real intention to interfere with slavery in the South. You could help convey this message. You can also comfort southern states by assuring them that Northerners could not end slavery in the South even if they wanted to because doing so would require an amendment to the Constitution. But constitutional amendments require ratification by three-fourths of the states. With 15 slave states in the Union voting against such an amendment, it could not possibly pass.

Even if your efforts to unite the states fail, history cannot fault you for doing everything in your power to stave off the crisis.

YOU ARE THE PRESIDENT.
WHAT IS YOUR DECISION?

Option 1   Let the states secede and abandon federal forts in those states.

Option 2   Send an army to bring the seceding states back into the Union.

Option 3   Allow the states to secede but hold on to the forts.

Option 4   Organize a national convention to find a compromise solution.

During his last days in office, President James Buchanan (1791-1868) had to decide whether states had the right to leave the Union.

President James Buchanan selected *Option 3*.

Buchanan decided that secession was illegal under the Constitution. But neither he nor anyone in his administration wanted to fight a war to preserve the Union. While refusing to recognize the rights of states to secede, the president also declared that the federal government would not force any state to remain in the Union.

Urging peaceful action, the president suggested that Congress call for a national convention to work out a solution that would keep the Union together. But he failed to use his influence as president to organize the convention or make a serious effort to bring the two factions together. In fact, Buchanan alienated the North beyond any hope of compromise.

Although Buchanan came from the northern state of Pennsylvania, he sympathized with the South in most matters. He blamed the present crisis on the "long continued intemperate interference of the northern people with the question of slavery." Buchanan said that if the North did not leave the South alone, the South would be justified in resisting.

At the same time, Buchanan recognized that he would commit political suicide and violate his oath of office if he surrendered the federal forts. As he told his secretary of war, if the forts were lost "in consequence of our neglect to put them in defensible condition . . . [it would be] better for you and me both to be thrown into the Potomac with millstones tied about our necks."

As much as he sought to avoid war, Buchanan could only hope the South would not attack the forts. If they did, war would be almost certain. "It will not then be a question of coercing a State to remain in the Union, to which I am utterly opposed," Buchanan said, "but it will be a question of voluntarily precipitating a conflict of arms on her part." Yet he would not risk provoking an attack by sending reinforcements to the forts.

Buchanan prayed that cool heads would prevail until the seceding states recognized the error of their ways and voluntarily returned to the Union.

RESULT

President Buchanan's policy pleased no one. Many Northerners were angry with him for not using force to bring the seceding states back into the Union, and Secretary of State Lewis Cass resigned because Buchanan failed to reinforce the forts. Southerners also turned

James Buchanan appointed Lewis Cass (1782-1866) to the position of U.S. secretary of state in 1857, but Cass resigned in December 1860 to protest Buchanan's refusal to reinforce the southern forts after several states seceded.

against him because he would neither surrender the forts nor accept secession as legal.

Although the seceding states refused to tolerate federal forts on their land, they were not ready to move against the forts during Buchanan's presidency. When Lincoln took over, he attempted to send limited reinforcements to Fort Sumter off the coast of Charleston, South Carolina. Before those supplies could land, shore-based artillery from Charleston opened fire on the ships and the fort. The bombardment forced the under-strength federal garrison at Fort Sumter to surrender.

Forces from Fort Moultrie attack Fort Sumter in Charleston Harbor on April 12, 1861.

This illustration from the May 4, 1861, cover of Harper's Weekly *shows residents of Charleston, South Carolina, on their rooftops watching the bombardment of Fort Sumter.*

This affront so outraged the North that it enthusiastically supported Lincoln in his call for federal armies to put down the rebellion. This response, in turn, prompted four more slave states to join the Confederate States of America. From that point, a brutal, all-out civil war was inevitable.

Republican newspapers claimed Buchanan could have stopped the war before it ever began if he had brought force against the South, like Andrew Jackson had done. Such a claim, however, ignores the widespread and deep-seated nature of Southern resentment toward the North.

Historians agree that a national convention to resolve the differences probably would have made little difference by the time the states had actually seceded. Both sides held so strongly to their beliefs that compromise was unlikely. In the absence of compromise, Buchanan preferred to let the seceding states go their own way rather than risk war. Had he simply abandoned the forts, only seven states would have seceded. Without a direct attack by the South on a federal fort to stir northern passions, Lincoln would have had a more difficult time getting the support he needed to proceed with the Civil War.

At the end of his life, Buchanan declared that he had "no regret for any public act of my life." Whether that statement reflected his honesty or his stubbornness, his policy regarding secession brought him nothing but anguish. It caused the South, whom he had so long defended, to abandon him. It also brought him a torrent of abuse, including reams of insulting and threatening letters, from Northerners throughout the war.

Historians have been similarly harsh in judging Buchanan's actions. Biographer Eldon Smith sums up the former president's performance by saying, "No president ever had better intentions than James Buchanan. Few have done more to frustrate their own objectives."

6

SLAVERY
July 1862

The bloody civil war that former president James Buchanan had sought to avoid is now taking place. The North insists that the South's act of secession is illegal according to the Constitution that governs the United States. The North is fighting to preserve the Union under that Constitution, while the South is fighting for the honor and independence of the slave-holding states.

With the southern states no longer taking part in the affairs of the federal government, your northern-dominated government now has the power to proceed as it wishes in the matter of slavery. You must decide how to handle this complicated issue without forgetting that your foremost responsibility is to get the Union back together somehow.

BACKGROUND

Black African slaves have been a part of American life for more than 200 years. The first shipload of slaves reached North America in 1619, one year before the Pilgrims reached the North American coast on the *Mayflower*. By the end of the eighteenth century, slaves proved to be especially valuable as field workers on the large farms and plantations of the South.

Eventually many Americans came to view the practice of slavery with disgust. Following the American Revolution in the late eighteenth century, the coastal states north of Delaware abolished slavery. In 1807, Congress outlawed the importation of slaves into the United States. Those who were already slaves, however, remained slaves, as did their children.

For the most part, those states that abolished slavery were those with the least to lose from such an action. With smaller farms and more heavily populated industrial areas, the North has little use for slaves. In the South, meanwhile, the institution of slavery has lasted so long and grown so large that it has become a major economic factor. Presently, about 4 million black slaves live in the South. Rightly or wrongly, these slaves are legal property. They represent an enormous investment by several generations of southern landowners.

The war started because Southerners feared the loss of both their property and their established way of life. Many white Southerners are also firmly convinced that blacks are inferior people whose proper function in society is to work as slaves. If you have any doubts about

During the early years of the United States, slave traders brought African slaves to North America by the shipload.

the importance of slavery to this war, Robert Rhett, one of the most influential public figures in South Carolina, has erased all doubt. "If we are not fighting for slavery," he has proclaimed, "what are we fighting for?"

The conflict, however, is not neatly divided between the proslavery South and the antislavery North. Between the two lie the border states of Delaware, Maryland, Kentucky, and Missouri. Because these states tend to be proslavery and loyal to the Union, their sympathies are divided.

Maryland and Kentucky are key states in your effort to hold the Union together. If Kentucky joins the rebel movement, it would strengthen the already formidable Confederate army and expand the territory of the Confederacy to the borders of the Great Lakes states. If Maryland secedes, the rebel states would virtually surround the Union capital of Washington, D.C., and the United States would probably have to abandon its governmental headquarters. Such a move would graphically demonstrate to the North the immense cost of forcing the seceding states back into the Union. It could end the war and destroy the Union you are trying to preserve.

There are indications that these border states are wavering in their devotion to the Union. Pro-southern mobs in the city of Baltimore have attacked northern troops traveling to Washington, D.C., and the Maryland legislature has voted to spend $500,000 to defend Baltimore from federal troops. In turn, Union soldiers have arrested 30 Maryland legislators and are enforcing martial law in some areas.

Kentucky is especially sensitive to the slave issue. More than 60 percent of its legislators own slaves. Its governor has stated, "Kentucky will furnish no troops for the wicked purpose of subduing her sister Southern states."

Nor is the North solidly opposed to slavery or supportive of the rights of blacks. White Northerners are not universal admirers of the black race. Much of the opposition to extending slave rights into the territories is actually racist. Many Westerners migrating into these areas simply do not want black people of any kind admitted.

THE DECISION IS YOURS.

What do you do about the issue of slavery?

Option 1 Immediately free all slaves as a matter of principle.

The enslavement of one group of people by another is barbaric. The nations of Europe have outlawed the practice. How then can the United States, a nation that prides itself on standing for the highest ideals of individual liberty, allow slavery to continue within its borders?

For more than 40 years, Northerners have tried to reason and compromise with southern slaveholders. Recently the Republicans have done almost everything possible to accommodate the South. They repeatedly assured the South that, as much as they abhor slavery, they would not interfere with slavery in the South.

Events of the past year have shown the futility of trying to appease the slaveholders. They have responded by illegally breaking away from the Union and triggering a terrible civil war. The policy of accommodating this small special-interest group has led the nation to the brink of ruin. (Fewer than ten percent of the white population in the South owns slaves.)

Concerns over whether an antislavery stance will offend the border states are just more of the same jelly-spined fears that have brought the nation to this sorry state. A nation that will not stand up for its ideals is not worth defending. Black leader Frederick Douglass puts the matter clearly: "If the Union can be maintained only

Frederick Douglass (1817-1895), an abolitionist speaker and writer, escaped from slavery in 1838 and lived much of his life as a fugitive slave.

by new concessions to the slaveholders," he said, "let the Union perish and perish forever."

The time has come for a bold, new approach. As black leader H. Ford Douglass III of Illinois says, "The very best way to overthrow slavery in this country is to occupy the highest possible anti-slavery ground." Since you cannot change the slaveholders' minds on this issue, you might as well take a firm stand for what is right and end this disgraceful practice of slavery at once.

Option 2 Leave the issue alone and concentrate on winning the war.

Regardless of your personal feelings about slavery, your foremost job as president is to protect and defend the Constitution of the United States. Former Supreme Court justice Benjamin Curtis argued that you cannot

Benjamin Curtis, who served on the Supreme Court from 1851 to 1857, believed that the U.S. president did not have the authority to free the slaves.

free the slaves without violating your oath and assuming powers that the Constitution does not give you. Only Congress has the power to make changes in the basic laws of the United States. By making yourself a dictator who sets his own laws, you do nothing to promote liberty in this country.

Above all, you must remember that your goal in fighting this war is to restore the Union. Freeing the slaves will not achieve that goal. In fact, it would do the opposite. It would drive a wedge between antislavery and proslavery supporters of the Union.

This action would have especially grave consequences in the border states. Last year, General John Frémont nearly caused the border states to bolt to the South while he was commanding the Union army in Missouri. Frémont declared he would free the slaves of anyone who took "an active part" with the Confederacy.

The famous explorer and former presidential candidate General John C. Frémont (1813-1890) was a zealous opponent of slavery.

Upon hearing this, Union volunteers from Kentucky immediately threw down their arms and refused to fight for the Union. This gives you a good indication of what might happen in the border states if you tried to free the slaves. If Kentucky and Maryland go over to the Confederacy, your chances of winning this war and saving the Union are slim.

Furthermore, such a proclamation may erode your support in the North. Although many white Northerners do not approve of slavery, most of them do not view blacks as their social equals. In fact, many northern communities already have strict laws segregating blacks from whites. They believe that the United States was formed as a nation for whites and was not meant to include black citizens. They are fearful that the abolition of slavery will release a horde of former slaves descending on the North. Northerners do not want what they view as uneducated, uncivilized, inferior beings upsetting their society.

Those who advocate freeing the slaves in the rebelling southern states claim this is an emergency military measure needed to save the Union. But even the commander of your armies, General George McClellan, disputes this. McClellan has written, "It should not be at all a war upon a population. . . . Neither confiscation of property . . . or forcible abolition of slavery should be contemplated for the moment."

Option 3 **Gradually phase out slavery with compensation to slave owners.**

Those who support slavery use three major arguments: 1) They back southern political leader Jefferson Davis in his claim that "the proper condition of the negro is slavery" by the "decree of Almighty God." 2) They agree that slaveholders have made a substantial property investment in slaves and that the government has no right to deprive the owners of their personal property. 3) They fear that a sudden end to slavery would have a disastrous effect on society.

Jefferson Davis (1808-1889), who was inaugurated as president of the Confederate States in Richmond, Virginia, in February 1862, argued for the expansion of slavery.

There is nothing you can do to dissuade the pro-slavery crowd from the first argument, but you can take steps to dispel the other two. While freeing the slaves, the government can offer to compensate slave owners for their property loss. In effect, the government would buy the slaves and set them free. In that way, the freeing of slaves would not cause economic hardship or deprive people of property.

The government can use the effects of time to calm fears that the end of slavery would have a disastrous impact on society. By freeing the slaves gradually over a period of 50 years or so, you would give the states ample time to prepare for and meet the challenges of a free black population that is currently poorly educated and impoverished.

This policy would face opposition from two quarters. Northerners will not be thrilled about their hard-earned tax money going to slave owners to buy slaves, especially during the harsh conditions of war. As one northern congressman complains, "The people of my district will not be taxed to purchase Negroes while the wives and children of our gallant soldiers are starving." Also, many slave owners scoff at the idea of compensation for their slaves. They view the plan as a bribe to get them to sell out their fellow Southerners.

Yet over time, as the weight of world opinion continues to turn against slavery, these attitudes will change. In the long run, this policy will prove the safer, surer way of ending slavery.

Option 4 **Free only the slaves in the rebelling states.**

Your foremost duty as president is to preserve the Union. Ulysses Grant, one of your generals who is operating in Kentucky, put it well when he assured the populace there by saying, "I have nothing to do with opinions. I shall deal only with armed rebellion and its aiders and abettors."

Under the current circumstance, a general emancipation of all slaves is both unconstitutional and, because of its effect on the border states, dangerous to the Union as well. But a limited emancipation may be an excellent tactic with which to fight the South.

Normal rules do not apply in emergencies. In times of war, a government assumes the right to destroy or confiscate enemy property so as to diminish the enemy's ability to fight. Black slaves in Confederate states are enemy property. After all, no one can deny that the 4 million slaves in the South provide the rebelling states with a considerable work force that helps the rebels to wage war on the United States. Therefore, the Union army has a legitimate interest in taking them from the enemy. Granting freedom to slaves of rebelling states would, therefore, be allowable under the Constitution.

Beyond a doubt, many of these slaves would welcome the chance to fight for their freedom. Thus, freeing the slaves in the rebelling states would not only deprive the South of their effort, it could also provide valuable troops and workers for the Union army.

This option would strike a severe blow to the rebels in the South and provide humanitarian relief to many black slaves. But this policy would not affect the slave owners in loyal Union states such as Kentucky and Maryland. Since the goal of the option is simply to thwart the rebels and preserve the Union, the border slave states would not feel threatened and would remain in the Union.

YOU ARE THE PRESIDENT. WHAT IS YOUR DECISION?

Option 1   Immediately free all slaves as a matter of principle.

Option 2   Leave the issue alone and concentrate on winning the war.

Option 3   Gradually phase out slavery with compensation to slave owners.

Option 4   Free only the slaves in the rebelling states.

President Abraham Lincoln (1809-1865) agonized for weeks over how to handle the issue of slavery.

President Abraham Lincoln chose *Option 4*.

"If slavery is not wrong, nothing is wrong," said Lincoln. "Yet I have never understood that the Presidency conferred upon me an unrestricted right to act officially upon this judgment." He saw that the Constitution gave the duty of making laws to Congress, not to the president.

In abiding by the limits of his office, Lincoln at first encouraged compromise and a gradual, long-term solution. He urged the government to compensate those slave owners who gave up their slaves, and he tried to marshal support for a plan that would gradually end slavery by the year 1900. But he stated clearly that the "paramount object in this struggle is to save the Union, it is not either to save or destroy slavery."

By the summer of 1862, Lincoln's hopes of saving the Union were dimming. Union forces in Virginia suffered defeat after disastrous defeat. The loss of life experienced in the apparently hopeless cause of forcing the South to return to the Union appalled the North. Support for Lincoln's war effort was eroding.

At this point, the president could no longer resist the military advantages of freeing the slaves in the rebelling states. As he later explained, "I was driven to the alternative of either surrendering the Union and with it the Constitution . . . or laying a strong hand upon the colored element. I chose the latter."

To those who complained that he had no constitutional right to declare slaves free, Lincoln answered that "measures otherwise unconstitutional might become lawful by becoming indispensable to the preserving of the Union." He emphasized that his proclamation "has no constitutional or legal justification, except as a military measure."

When some of his advisers protested that he had rebuked Frémont for doing the same thing just a year ago, Lincoln admitted he had changed his mind. "I don't think much of a man who is not wiser today than he was yesterday," he said. William Seward, Lincoln's secretary of state, thought a proclamation freeing the slaves would sound like an idle threat, given the hapless performance of the Union army. So Lincoln agreed to wait until the army gained a victory before issuing his Emancipation Proclamation.

Secretary of State William Seward watches President Lincoln sign the Emancipation Proclamation.

In September, following fierce yet indecisive fighting at the battle of Antietam, Confederate armies retreated. Lincoln accepted this as a victory. On September 22, 1862, he announced that, as of January 1, 1863, "all persons held as slaves within any state, or designated part of a state, the people whereof shall then be in rebellion against the United States, shall be then, thenceforward, and forever free."

RESULT

The proclamation sent tremors of fear and outrage throughout the North as well as the South. The Illinois state legislature branded Lincoln's decision an "uneffaceable disgrace to the American people, the consequences of which for both races cannot be contemplated without the most dismal foreboding of horror and dismay."

Many people feared that the announcement strengthened the cause of the rebels and expected the border slave states to join the Confederacy. Horace Greeley, editor of the *New York Tribune*, wrote that Lincoln's proclamation drove home "the wedge intended to divide the union."

The pessimists, however, were wrong. None of the border states turned against the Union, and Lincoln's tact in declining to interfere with slavery in the border states paid off. The black press in the North greeted Lincoln's act with enthusiasm. Responding to regrets that the act freed slaves only in rebelling states, one writer declared, "We believe those who are not immediately liberated will be ultimately benefited by the act."

In his August 19, 1862, editorial entitled "The Prayer of Twenty Millions," New York Tribune editor Horace Greeley demanded that President Lincoln free the slaves.

As Lincoln had expected, the Emancipation Proclamation greatly aided the Union cause. It robbed the South of considerable human resources and put thousands of blacks actively at work for the North. An estimated 50,000 slaves joined General Grant during his campaign at Chattanooga alone, and more than 38,000 black Union soldiers died in action. Late in the war, Lincoln wrote, "Take from us and give to the enemy the 130, 140, 150 thousand colored persons now serving us as soldiers, seamen and laborers, and we cannot longer maintain the contest."

This poster was used to encourage blacks to join the Union army during the Civil War.

HINDSIGHT

Lincoln never regretted his decision. "Right or wrong, I assumed this ground and now avow it," he wrote near the end of the war. He always justified it as a military decision whose purpose was to restore the Union, not as a social action.

But while the Emancipation Proclamation did help achieve a Union victory, it accomplished far more than that. The bold action of freeing the slaves in the South triggered a landslide of public opinion that buried the practice of slavery once and for all. As further vindication of Lincoln's policy, the greatest momentum for this change came in the border states that Lincoln had spared from his proclamation. One political observer noted that within a year of the Emancipation Proclamation, the border states of Missouri and Maryland, "neither of which three years ago would tolerate any restraint upon the extension of slavery into new territories, only dispute now as to the best mode of removing it from their limits."

Even before the end of the war, the institution of slavery was dying in the South. The necessities of war forced Confederate generals to recruit black soldiers by promising them freedom. Once the door of freedom had been opened, there was no shutting it.

On December 18, 1865, Congress tossed the final shovelful on the grave of slavery by passing the Thirteenth Amendment outlawing the practice in all the United States. Only one congressman from a border state voted against the amendment.

Lincoln's secretaries John Hay and John Nicolay summed up the conclusions of many when they described the Emancipation Proclamation as "one of the greatest and most beneficent military decrees of history."

7

HAWAII
Summer 1893

No sooner did you take office in March than you found a gut-churning diplomatic problem waiting for you on the Pacific islands of Hawaii.

Slightly fewer than half the inhabitants of these islands are native Hawaiians. The rest are a mixture of Chinese, Portuguese, Japanese, German, and American settlers. Although the Americans make up about five percent of the population, they control most of the islands' commercial interests.

Until now, the traditional Hawaiian government under Queen Liliuokalani had ruled Hawaii. But in January a group of American businessmen living in Hawaii staged a revolt. These revolutionaries formed a new government and immediately requested annexation by the United States. This would make Hawaii a territory under U.S. protection, but not officially a state. The previous U.S. president, Benjamin Harrison, granted that request. In February, he arranged a treaty of annexation and submitted it to the U.S. Senate for approval.

The Senate, however, had not acted on that treaty by the time you took office. After hearing disturbing reports that unauthorized U.S. troops participated in the revolt, you sent former congressman James Blount to Hawaii on a fact-finding mission. Blount confirmed that an official of the U.S. government had played a key role in the government takeover. Blount further reports that a large majority of the islanders oppose annexation. In light of this information, you must decide what policy you will pursue toward Hawaii.

James Blount (1837-1903), who served as the president's special commissioner to Hawaii in 1893, argued against the provisional government.

President Benjamin Harrison (1833-1901) thought the Hawaiian islands, located more than 2,000 miles southwest of California, were too far away for the United States to govern successfully.

BACKGROUND

As the United States tries to increase its overseas commerce, the small islands of Hawaii in the Pacific Ocean take on greater importance. These islands stand as a welcome outpost to ships making the long voyage from Asia to the North American continent. Their location on a long, narrow, vital shipping lane makes the islands both a center of trade and a valuable military property.

The United States has maintained a treaty of friendship and commerce with the kingdom of Hawaii; the United States has worked hard to secure both its commercial and military advantages. In 1887, the United States gained permission to build a naval base at Pearl Harbor on the island of Oahu.

The American revolutionaries who plotted the takeover, led by wealthy planter Sanford Dole, grew increasingly frustrated with Queen Liliuokalani. They viewed her as a primitive tyrant who was intent on violating the Hawaiian Constitution that protected the rights of the white minority. They believed her ignorance of modern commerce was destroying the economic base they had labored so hard to build up.

Dole and his supporters, however, made no move to overthrow the government until they received secret approval from John L. Stevens, the U.S. minister to Hawaii. Acting without authorization from the United States government, Stevens provided military support to the plotters. When the revolt started, he ordered naval marines ashore to "protect the lives and property of United States citizens." The marines occupied key government buildings. Their presence thwarted the efforts of the queen's loyalists to maintain control of the government. Dole's group declared itself the new provisional government of Hawaii and placed Queen Liliuokalani under virtual house arrest. Stevens immediately recognized Dole's government and declared Hawaii to be under the protection of the United States.

Sanford Dole (1844-1926), a native of Honolulu and president of the provisional government, believed that Hawaii's previous political system had become ineffective and outdated.

Acting under the authority of John L. Stevens, the U.S. minister to Hawaii, American troops guard the front of Hawaii's judiciary building.

THE DECISION IS YOURS.

What action will you take concerning annexation of Hawaii?

Option 1 **Annex Hawaii.**

While Stevens may have acted improperly by calling in the marines to support the revolt, matters have actually worked out for the best. You have a strong interest in Hawaii for military, political, and economic reasons. The islands may seem far away from the United States, but if they fell into enemy hands, they could provide a base from which a foreign power could attack the California coast. There are no suitable islands between Hawaii and California that could provide the United States with a defensive base from which to intercept this attack.

This is no idle fear. Germany, for example, has been aggressively trying to acquire Pacific islands. A few years ago, Germany nearly provoked a war with the United States by attempting to gain control of Samoa. You must also be alert to the possibility that Japan, a growing military power, might expand eastward into the Pacific.

Politically, Queen Liliuokalani is a dangerous, incompetent tyrant—the kind of ruler that freedom-loving Americans have always opposed. Her firm belief in her right to behead those she regards as her enemies clearly illustrates her primitive style of leadership. The queen is so far behind the times that she cannot possibly hope to govern effectively. As long as she continues to rule over a large and wealthy minority, Hawaii will be ripe for revolution. Revolutions can be far messier than this one proved to be, so you are better off leaving matters as they stand. If you put her back in power, you would do nothing more than postpone Hawaii's problems for a later generation to solve.

Queen Liliuokalani, who ascended to the throne in 1891, is remembered for demanding that other nations leave "Hawaii for the Hawaiians!"

Economically, Hawaii's prime location makes it a key center of international trade. With Dole's government in power, trade will be especially favorable to Americans. At this moment, the United States is plunging into a severe economic depression. Risking the loss of a thriving U.S. economic outpost would hardly help this situation.

Option 2 **Reject annexation and order the restoration of Queen Liliuokalani's government.**

The honor of the United States is at stake. Without receiving any authority from the U.S. government, Stevens schemed and plotted with his American friends on the island to destroy the legitimate government of Hawaii. No strategic interest can possibly justify the blatant interference of the United States into the internal affairs of a foreign country.

Secretary of State Walter Gresham argues strongly for restoring Queen Liliuokalani to the throne. He has described the conduct of John L. Stevens as shameful. Gresham says that by ordering those actions in the name of the United States, Stevens made the United States an accomplice in his crime.

Historically, the United States has tried to stand on principles of individual liberty and freedom. Gresham cuts to the heart of the matter when he asks, "Should not the great wrong done to a feeble but independent State by an abuse of the authority of the U.S. government be undone by restoring the legitimate government?"

Furthermore, the American citizens in Hawaii are not the poor, persecuted minority that they make themselves out to be. Dole and his supporters are greedy people who are looking out only for their own interests. Although the small percentage of Americans already own most of the island's wealth, they are looking for a way to pile up even bigger profits. They want to gain control of the government so they can dictate laws that will favor them. One of the main reasons they support annexation is because they know the U.S. government provides price supports to American sugar growers. If Hawaii becomes part of the United States, Hawaiian sugar growers will share in that handout.

The only way the United States can restore its reputation is to undo the injustice it has caused and return the situation to what it was before Stevens interfered.

Option 3 Reject annexation and leave Hawaii to solve its own problems.

Stevens's actions on behalf of the U.S. government were unforgivable. Therefore, you must not tarnish the United States by accepting stolen property. On the other hand, you cannot turn back the clock and restore everything to the way it had been. Given Queen Liliuokalani's past behavior and present outrage, restoring her to her throne would seal the death sentence of many Americans in Hawaii. The queen vows to cut off the heads of any who took any part in the revolt.

Attorney General Richard Olney warns you that, although you must be concerned about the injustice done to the queen's government, you must also concern yourself with "securing justice and fair play for the provisional government" of Sanford Dole. These people are, after all, U.S. citizens. You have an obligation to help them protect their lives and their property from the whims of foreign rulers.

The two sides in Hawaii have shown no interest in compromising. The Dole government refuses to give up power voluntarily, and forcing it to do so would require sending U.S. troops to fight on the side of a foreign nation against U.S. citizens. Such a scenario would probably outrage many Americans. Then, after your troops fought Dole and forced him out, they would probably have to stay in Hawaii to protect American citizens from the queen's forces.

Chances are good that the islands would erupt in civil war long before you got matters straightened out. The last thing you want is for the United States to provoke a civil war and then get caught in the middle of the crossfire.

Option 4 **Supervise popular elections to determine which government Hawaii wants and whether it wishes annexation.**

The United States can help solve the chaos in Hawaii's government by encouraging democracy. If the United States truly believes its longstanding principle that government should reflect the will of the people, then it will help Hawaii establish a government that does just that.

The United States should not use its power either to stir up trouble by toppling Dole's government and reinstating Queen Liliuokalani or to fight the queen's attempts at revenge. Rather, it should use this power to supervise fair elections among the Hawaiian people. These elections will determine what form of government the Hawaiians' desire and whom they prefer to lead them. James Blount reports that a large majority of Hawaiians do not favor annexation. These elections would prove or disprove this once and for all.

This option protects U.S. interests by ensuring the stability of a nation with which it is already on good terms. The United States can further protect its interests by assuming temporary control over the islands. This control would favor neither Dole nor Queen Liliuokalani. Such a policy would encourage both sides to participate in a peaceful solution to their problems and would prevent any foreign powers from moving in to take advantage of the disorder.

YOU ARE THE PRESIDENT.
WHAT IS YOUR DECISION?

Option 1   **Annex Hawaii.**

Option 2   **Reject annexation and order the restoration of Queen Liliuokalani's government.**

Option 3   **Reject annexation and leave Hawaii to solve its own problems.**

Option 4   **Supervise popular elections to determine which government Hawaii wants and whether it wishes annexation.**

President Grover Cleveland (1837-1908) had to decide whether Queen Liliuokalani or Sanford Dole should rule Hawaii.

President Grover Cleveland chose *Option 3*.

Cleveland generally tried to do what was morally right rather than merely what was in the best interests of the United States. In March 1893, he said that if the United States were ever to annex Hawaii, the action must clearly be the will of the Hawaiian people and free from any pressure from officials of the U.S. government.

Even in that case, Cleveland said "we ought to stop and look and think" before agreeing to annex the islands. Unlike the previous administration of President Benjamin Harrison, Cleveland opposed expanding the borders of the United States, especially as far away from North America as Hawaii. He did not like the idea of powerful nations absorbing small, weak countries. If the United States started doing this, other nations might try some empire-building of their own.

Blount's report easily persuaded Cleveland that the request for annexation came from a small special-interest group on the islands and not from the majority of the people. The president, therefore, rejected annexation.

Furthermore, the role of Stevens and the U.S. marines in the revolt disturbed Cleveland. He agreed with Secretary of State Gresham's conclusion that the unauthorized and wrongful use of U.S. military force was responsible for putting the Dole government in power. The president believed the United States had to answer for that action.

But Cleveland also sympathized with Attorney General Olney's views that cautioned against further military involvement. Fearful of inciting a civil war in

Hawaii and of provoking a hostile reaction in the United States by sending troops to fight Americans in Hawaii, Cleveland took no action against Dole's government. He concluded that the United States had no more business sending troops to restore the queen's position than it had in becoming involved in the first place.

In his address to the nation, Cleveland approached the situation cautiously. He said, "If a feeble but friendly state is in danger of being robbed of its independence and its sovereignty by a misuse of the name and power of the United States, the United States cannot fail to vindicate its honor and its sense of justice by an earnest effort to make all possible reparation."

For President Cleveland, that effort consisted solely of trying to persuade the Dole government to resign and the queen to treat the revolters leniently.

RESULT

Neither Queen Liliuokalani nor Dole budged from their previous positions. The queen continued to threaten violence, and the leaders of the new government refused Cleveland's request that they resign. Dole, who had used the United States to gain power, now professed outrage at the "interference" of the U.S. government in the internal affairs of Hawaii.

Unable to negotiate a solution and unwilling to send troops, Cleveland dumped the problem in Congress's lap. In May 1894, after much debate, Congress passed a resolution that advised the president to recognize Dole's group as the legitimate government of Hawaii. Cleveland reluctantly agreed. He went so far as to compliment Dole publicly and to wish him "personal prosperity" in the new Republic of Hawaii.

Dole's government remained in power after Cleveland left office. The new president, William McKinley, then recommended that the United States annex Hawaii. The Senate confirmed his wish on July 6, 1898, and Hawaii became the property of the United States. Hawaii joined the Union as the 50th U.S. state on August 21, 1959.

After failing to regain her throne in 1895, Queen Liliuokalani (1838-1917) formally renounced all of her royal claims to rule Hawaii.

HINDSIGHT

Cleveland was primarily concerned with steering a course that upheld the nation's honor. He also wanted to prevent the United States from expanding into the Pacific Ocean. But he failed on both counts. Cleveland's policy resulted in the United States recognizing an illegal government that had used the power of the United States to seize control. There was no honor in that. His efforts to prevent expansion into the Pacific did nothing but delay the annexation of Hawaii for five years.

Historian R. Hal Williams describes Cleveland's Hawaiian policy as "a mixture of admirable principle and blundering naivete." The president recognized that agents of the United States had acted dishonorably, and he forthrightly exposed the deceit. But he could find no way to undo the damage.

Cleveland's policy of trying to "make reparations" to Queen Liliuokalani's government without the use of force was, according to biographer Richard Welch, Jr., little more than wishful thinking. In the end, Cleveland could only shrug his shoulders and leave the matter to Congress. This, says Welch, was a shirking of his responsibility "and, in the end, a mistake."

8

THE CUBAN REBELLION
April 1898

For the past three years, the people of the United States have been intensely concerned about the island of Cuba off the southern coast of Florida. In 1895, only 17 years after the failure of a bloody, 10-year revolt, the Cuban people launched another desperate war for independence from their Spanish masters.

Aside from the fact that this war flares so close to the U.S. border, Americans have good reason to be wary of the Cuban crisis. U.S. citizens own a considerable share of the Cuban plantations, which produce more sugar than any other place in the world. Many Americans depend on the thriving trade between the United States and Cuba for their livelihood.

Nor is the U.S. interest in Cuba likely to fade as long as an active group of Cuban nationals in the United States is fanning the flames of freedom. These Cubans have effectively conveyed a heartbreaking picture of their suffering under Spanish rule.

Over the past three years, public opinion in the United States has steadily swung in favor of the Cuban rebels. While taking no part in the conflict, the U.S. government has urged Spain to relax its grip on Cuba. While insisting that the United States has no business interfering in Cuba, Spain has made grudging concessions to the Cubans.

In February, a shocking incident raised the Cuban situation to the crisis stage. An American battleship, the USS *Maine*, exploded while docked in Havana, Cuba, on a peaceful mission. At least 260 American sailors died in the blast. Two weeks ago, a U.S. naval court concluded that a submerged mine caused the blast. Spain is the obvious suspect in this apparent act of murder and sabotage, and many Americans are now calling for war against Spain.

BACKGROUND

The Spanish flag once flew over the lands from the southern parts of North America to South America. But the nation long ago lost its status as a major world power. Centuries of mismanagement and bad fortune have robbed Spain of its wealth and its colonies, and Cuba and the small island of Puerto Rico are all that remain of

After the battleship Maine *exploded in Havana harbor on February 15, 1898, "Remember the Maine!" became a popular slogan that was used to promote hostility toward Spain.*

the once-proud Spanish empire in the Americas. Shamed by their fall from power, the Spanish cling fiercely to the last of their possessions. Despite the strain this puts on their meager national treasury, they have committed a quarter of a million soldiers to defending Cuba.

The outgunned Cuban rebels have fought an effective fight-and-hide (guerrilla) campaign against Spain. The Spanish concluded that the best way to stop the rebels was to cut off their support in the local villages and farms. Under General Valeriano Weyler, Spanish forces burned crops and homes, then herded all the rural Cubans into concentration camps along the coast. This ruthless policy has brought famine and disease to hundreds of thousands of Cuban civilians. Reliable observers estimate that at least 200,000 from a total population of 1.5 million have died in these concentration camps.

Horror stories of these camps have triggered American outrage against Spain. Resentful of American criticism, the Spanish people argue that the United States invented the disastrous practice of fighting a civil war during its own. The Spanish also point out that the rebels themselves have been burning plantations and Spanish property for years. Nonetheless, under U.S. pressure, Spain has recently made humanitarian concessions. It has agreed to allow Cuba some sort of self-rule under the Spanish flag and has finally agreed to disband the concentration camps. The Cubans, though, insist on complete freedom from Spain.

Spain has reason to fear American involvement in Cuba. The fortunes of the United States have risen as dramatically as those of Spain have fallen. Within a century, the U.S. has expanded from a struggling collection of states on the eastern seaboard to a wealthy nation that spans the width of the continent. Most observers are convinced that Spain is no match for the United States in warfare.

The Spanish, however, hope that aid from their allies will even the odds. The major powers of Europe—Great Britain, France, Germany, and Russia—generally sympathize with Spain in the Cuban conflict. Germany, which arrived late on the colonial scene, is especially interested in picking up some foreign territory and might be tempted to work out a deal with Spain. So far, however, none of the European nations have indicated its intent to support Spain militarily.

THE DECISION IS YOURS.

How do you handle this crisis in Cuba?

Option 1 Recognize the Cuban rebels and send humanitarian aid.

The Cuban revolution does not directly concern the United States and so you have no business taking any military action. But neither can you sit idly. Hundreds of thousands of Cubans are crying for freedom, and Spain's only response has been to inflict inhumane punishment on innocent civilians. You must at least provide moral and financial support.

If you have any doubt about the correctness of this option, you have only to listen to Senator Redfield Proctor of Vermont, who recently returned from a visit to Cuba. Proctor paints a graphic picture of "desolation and distress, misery and starvation." He describes an

Redfield Proctor (1831-1908) was one of the most vocal supporters of giving aid to Cuba.

endless cycle of deaths in the streets, and of children starving and dying from disease. Even if Spain abandons its concentration camps, the Spanish cannot undo the misery they have caused. The people of Cuba, says Proctor, are "struggling for freedom and deliverance from the worst misgovernment of which I ever had knowledge."

The United States must do all it can, short of war, to show its support for the ideals of liberty and justice on which it was founded.

Option 2 **Give recent Spanish concessions time to work.**

The Spanish queen asks you to give the recent Spanish concessions time to work. She wants you to hold off on any action until late in the summer. "By then," says the Spanish foreign minister, "we shall have reached an accommodation with the Cuban insurgents that will be acceptable to all parties and then there will be peace."

Stewart Woodford, the U.S. ambassador to Spain, agrees. He points out that, "public opinion in Spain has steadily moved toward peace." Spain's rulers are making all the concessions they can. If they yield to pressure to grant immediate freedom to Cuba, they will wound the pride of the Spanish people sufficiently to create a rebellion in Spain itself. The best policy is to wait and let

Spanish officials told Stewart Woodford, the U.S. ambassador to Spain, that they did not want to go to war against the United States.

reality sink in. The Spanish will soon realize the futility of trying to hold on to Cuba.

The waiting option presents many advantages. First, it keeps you out of a war that is not really your affair in the first place. Former president Ulysses Grant set a wise example by avoiding any interference in the first Cuban revolution, and you would do well to follow him. Second, this option avoids entanglement with the European powers. You know that the European nations do not approve of American meddling in Cuba. While you run little risk in taking action against Spain, you could find yourself in over your head if Germany and France come to Spain's rescue.

President Ulysses Grant (1822-1885), who served from 1869 to 1877, kept the United States out of Cuba's Ten Years War against Spain.

Finally, even if you decide to go to war against Spain, the climate of Cuba suggests that you would be wise to delay that action. More than one army has found the climate in that area to be far more deadly than enemy soldiers. If at all possible, you want to avoid fighting during Cuba's rainy season, which begins in less than two months. The rains make the heat and humidity unbearable and spawn tropical diseases that could decimate your forces. While you are waiting for better weather, the Spanish concessions may have time to work.

Option 3 **Send troops to Cuba for the purpose of annexing the island.**

Many Americans over the years have wanted Cuba to be part of the United States. Former president John Quincy Adams referred to Cuba as a "natural appendage to the North American continent." According to Adams, "It is scarcely possible to resist the conviction that the annexation of Cuba to our federal republic will be indispensable."

Now is the time for the United States to bring Cuba into the fold. Cuba is in such a pathetic state of affairs that a U.S. takeover would be a humanitarian action. William J. Calhoun, whom you sent on an official fact-finding mission to Cuba, confirmed this. Finding little cause for hope on the island, Calhoun reported that while Spain had lost its ability to govern the island, Cuba was not ready for independence. The war had left the country in a state of extreme poverty and political chaos.

The utter breakdown of government in Cuba leaves a void that only a strong, stable power can fill. The

*John Quincy Adams (1767-1848), the sixth U.S.
president, was one of the nation's first political leaders
to say that Cuba should be linked to the United States.*

After returning to the United States from Cuba, William J. Calhoun felt that neither the Cubans nor the Spanish government were strong enough to govern the island.

United States is the logical choice to fill that void. Cuba, which is essentially in the United States' back yard, is a close trading partner. American business people have millions of dollars worth of property in Cuba that could be tied up or destroyed unless you can straighten out the mess on the island.

Although some people argue that you should concern yourself only with what goes on inside U.S. borders, the time has come for the United States to take its place in the world as a first-rate power. The United States should use that power to benefit the people of the world instead of standing aside while tyranny and disorder reign. If the United States neglects its duty toward Cuba, you can rest assured that some European power will come in to fill the void. It would not be in the best interest of Cuba or the United States to see Germany set up shop in the Caribbean. This action will mean war with Spain, but Spain is not a serious military threat.

Option 4 Send troops to fight for Cuban independence.

The United States, as a champion of liberty, cannot muscle its way in and claim lands governed by others. If the Cubans overwhelmingly request annexation, the United States can accommodate them. But the Cubans are not asking for this.

Nonetheless, the situation will only get worse unless the United States steps in and forces a settlement. The warring sides have no intention of compromising. Cubans will never agree to anything less than full independence. The Spanish army has already rioted over news that its government might offer a truce and possibly agree to limited self-government for Cuba.

Spain is far too passionate about holding on to Cuba, its last source of self-respect as a fading European power, to expect a change of attitude in the near future. One Spanish official put the issue plainly. "Understand this well. We cannot give up Cuba; we absolutely cannot." The apparent sabotage against the USS *Maine* shows to what lengths the Spanish will go to hold on to Cuba.

Such attitudes foreshadow a long and bloody struggle in Cuba, one that neither Cuba nor the United States can afford. Since the Spanish cannot resolve this situation, you must take military action to force them to leave. The consequences of inaction would be steep. Sentiment in the United States runs so heavily in favor of war that

Congress is likely to declare war whether you like it or not. If that happens, you could lose the respect of the American people. For your own political survival, your congressional allies urge you to "lead and not be pushed."

YOU ARE THE PRESIDENT.
WHAT IS YOUR DECISION?

Option 1   **Recognize the Cuban rebels and send humanitarian aid.**

Option 2   **Give recent Spanish concessions time to work.**

Option 3   **Send troops to Cuba for the purpose of annexing the island.**

Option 4   **Send troops to fight for Cuban independence.**

President William McKinley chose *Option 4*.

McKinley wanted desperately to avoid war. At the start of his term, he confided to outgoing President Cleveland, "If I can only go out of office at the end of my term, with the knowledge that I have done what lay in my power to avert this terrible calamity . . . I shall be the happiest man in the world."

For a brief time, McKinley held out hope that Spain could work out a peaceable settlement with the Cubans. In December 1897, he declared that Spain deserved a reasonable chance for its latest offer of limited self-government to gain support.

But within a month of that statement, the Spanish army and its supporters, outraged over the first small steps toward conciliation, rioted in Havana. This convinced McKinley that no amount of diplomacy could get Spain to admit it could no longer govern Cuba.

The president rejected recognition of the Cuban rebels for fear that "our conduct [in Cuba] would be subjected to the approval" of their new government. McKinley did not want his hands tied by a disorganized Cuban leadership that he did not entirely trust.

McKinley cited the famine in Cuba and the sabotage of the *Maine* as proof of Spain's dishonorable intentions there. He declared that the United States had exhausted every possible avenue of negotiated peace. Its patience was now at an end, and American military action was required.

McKinley understood the risk he was taking regarding a possible Spanish-European alliance. "Who knows

Although many Americans wanted to go to war against Spain, President William McKinley (1843-1901) wasn't positive that war was the best option.

where this war will lead us?" he said privately. "It may be more than war with Spain."

On April 11, 1898, the president asked Congress for the authority to use U.S. military forces to end Spanish rule in Cuba. "In the name of humanity, in the name of civilization, in behalf of endangered American interests which give us the right and the duty to speak and to act," said McKinley, "the war in Cuba must stop." He was willing to fight a war with Spain to end the war in Cuba.

U.S. soldiers on horseback prepare to battle Spanish forces in Cuba.

U.S. soldiers dig in against enemy troops during the Spanish-American War, which lasted from April to July 1898.

RESULT

The Spanish-American War lasted only three months. The Americans won every battle fought on both land and sea. By May 1, 1898, American warships had destroyed Spain's Pacific fleet in the Philippine Islands. In July, the U.S. Navy dealt a similar defeat to Spain's naval squadron in the Caribbean Sea. That same month, U.S. soldiers forced the Spanish surrender of the key Cuban fortifications at Santiago and cut through weak Spanish resistance on Puerto Rico. By the end of July, the fighting was over. This war marked the emergence of the United States as one of the dominant world powers.

The defeated Spanish not only agreed to grant independence to Cuba, they also surrendered the islands of Puerto Rico and Guam to the United States and sold the Philippine Islands for a bargain price of $20 million.

HINDSIGHT

Historians have hotly debated the merits of the Spanish-American War. Certainly the United States achieved its goals at a very low cost. The United States suffered fewer than 400 combat deaths in this brief war, although tropical diseases, particularly yellow fever, claimed the lives of more than 2,000 American soldiers. The American people enthusiastically supported the fight. John Hay, the U.S. ambassador to London, called it "a splendid little war, begun with the highest motives, carried on with magnificent intelligence and spirit, favored by that fortune which loves the brave."

On the other hand, many historians have called the war unnecessary. They believe that Spain was gradually, if grudgingly, moving on the road to peace. They often describe McKinley as a weak, indecisive leader who gave in to the demands of an irresponsible press, an over-emotional public, and land-hungry expansionists. As evidence of an irrational anti-Spanish mood in the country, they cite furor over the sinking of the USS *Maine*. A 1976 study by the U.S. Navy concluded that the damage was caused by an internal explosion, not a Spanish mine.

Biographer Lewis L. Gould believes that, while this was not exactly a "splendid war," McKinley deserves praise for his policy. Gould questions whether the rebels would have agreed to any plan short of total independence or that the Spanish would ever have offered this of their own free will. McKinley did resist the temptation to annex a people who did not want to be annexed.

Gould concludes, "McKinley's ability to postpone the war for as long as he did and to control the terms on which the U.S. commenced hostilities indicates that his presidential leadership . . . was more courageous and principled than his critics have realized."

SOURCE NOTES

Quoted passages are noted by page and order of citation:

pp. 9, 82, 83, 84 (1st), 86, 90, 91, 94: Elbert B. Smith, *The Presidency of James Buchanan* (Lawrence, KS: University of Kansas Press, 1975.)

pp. 20 (1st), 23, 25, 26 (1st): Forrest McDonald, *The Presidency of Thomas Jefferson* (Lawrence, KS: University of Kansas Press, 1976.)

pp. 20 (2nd), 26 (2nd, 3rd): Alf J. Mapp, Jr., *Thomas Jefferson: Passionate Pilgrim* (Lanham, MD: Madison Books, 1991.)

pp. 32, 33 (2nd, 3rd), 38, 41, 45, 46: Robert A. Rutland, *James Madison: The Founding Father* (New York: Macmillan, 1987.)

pp. 33 (1st), 35, 37: Harry L. Coles, *The War of 1812* (Chicago: University of Chicago Press, 1966.)

p. 49: Grant Foreman, *Indian Removal: The Emigration of the Five Civilized Tribes of Indians* (Norman, OK: University of Oklahoma, 1972.)

pp. 52, 57 (3rd, 4th): John Ehle, *Trail of Tears: The Rise and Fall of the Cherokee Nation* (New York, Doubleday, 1988.)

pp. 57 (1st, 2nd), 58, 59, 60, 84 (2nd), 85: Robert Remini, *Andrew Jackson and the Course of American Empire* (New York: Harper & Row, 1977.)

p. 67: Frederick Merk, *The Monroe Doctrine and American Expansionism: 1843-49* (New York: Knopf, 1972.)

p. 68 (1st): David Sievert Lavender, *Land of Giants: The Drive to the Pacific Northwest, 1750-1950* (New York: Doubleday, 1958.)

pp. 68 (2nd), 72 (1st), 75, 78: Paul H. Bergeron, *The Presidency of James K. Polk.* (Lawrence, KS: University of Kansas Press, 1987.)

p. 68 (3rd): Kingsley Bryce Smellie, *Great Britain Since 1688: A Modern History* (Ann Arbor: University of Michigan, 1962.)

pp. 72 (2nd): Margaret L. Coit, ed., *John C. Calhoun: Great Lives Observed* (Englewood Cliffs, NJ: Prentice Hall, 1970.)

pp. 98, 100, 101, 104, 105, 106, 109 (2nd), 110, 111 (2nd, 3rd): William O. Douglas, *Mr. Lincoln and the Negroes: The Long Road to Equality.* (New York: Atheneum, 1963.)

pp. 99, 109 (1st, 3rd, 4th), 111 (1st), 112, 113, 114: John Nicolay and John Hay, *Abraham Lincoln: A History* (Chicago: University of Chicago Press, 1966.)

pp. 118, 123, 124, 132: Richard E. Welch, Jr., *The Presidencies of Grover Cleveland* (Lawrence, Kansas: University of Kansas Press, 1988.)

pp. 128, 129, 130: Rexford G. Tugwell, *Grover Cleveland* New York: Macmillan, 1968.)

pp. 138, 145, 146, 148, 150: Lewis L. Gould, *The Presidency of William McKinley* (Lawrence, KS: Regents Press of Kansas, 1980.)

pp. 139, 141, 144, 146, 151: G. J. A. O'Toole, *The Spanish War: An American Epic, 1898* (New York: W. W. Norton, 1984.)

BIBLIOGRAPHY

Bergeron, Paul H. *The Presidency of James K. Polk.* Lawrence, KS: University of Kansas Press, 1987.

Carter, Alden, *The War of 1812.* New York: Franklin Watts, 1992.

Coit, Margaret, ed. *John C. Calhoun: Great Lives Observed.* Englewood Cliffs, NJ: Prentice Hall, 1970.

Coles, Harry L. *The War of 1812.* Chicago: University of Chicago Press, 1965.

Douglas, William O. *Mr. Lincoln and the Negroes: The Long Road to Equality.* New York: Atheneum, 1963.

Ehle, John. *Trail of Tears: The Rise and Fall of the Cherokee Nation.* New York: Doubleday, 1988.

Foreman, Grant. *Indian Removal: The Emigration of the Five Civilized Tribes of Indians.* Norman, OK: University of Oklahoma, 1972.

Gould, Lewis L. *The Presidency of William McKinley.* Lawrence, KS: Regents Press of Kansas, 1980.

Horsman, Reginald, *The War of 1812.* New York: Knopf, 1969.

King, Duane, H. *The Cherokee Indian Nation: A Troubled History.* Knoxville: University of Tennessee, 1978.

Lavender, David Sievert. *Land of Giants: The Drive to the Pacific Northwest, 1750-1950.* New York: Doubleday, 1958.

Mapp, Alf J., Jr. *Thomas Jefferson: Passionate Pilgrim.* Lanham, MD: Madison Books, 1991.

McDonald, Forrest. *The Presidency of Thomas Jefferson.* Lawrence, KS: University of Kansas Press, 1976.

McPherson, James M. *The Negroes' Civil War.* New York: Pantheon Books, 1965.

Merk, Frederick. *The Monroe Doctrine and American Expansionism: 1843-49.* New York: Knopf, 1972.

Nicolay, John and John Hay. *Abraham Lincoln: A History.* Chicago: University of Chicago, 1966.

O'Toole, G. J. A. *The Spanish War: An American Epic, 1898.* New York: W. W. Norton, 1984.

Randall, J.G. *Lincoln the President.* New York: Dodd, Mead, 1952.

Remini, Robert. *Andrew Jackson and the Course of American Empire.* New York: Harper & Row, 1977.

Rutland, Robert A. *James Madison: The Founding Father.* New York: Macmillan, 1987.

Smellie, Kingsley Bryce. *Great Britain Since 1688: A Modern History.* Ann Arbor: University of Michigan, 1962.

Smith, Elbert B. *The Presidency of James Buchanan.* Lawrence, Kansas: University of Kansas Press, 1975.

Sprague, Marshall. *So Vast and Beautiful a Land: Louisiana and the Purchase.* Boston: Little, Brown & Co., 1974.

Tugwell, Rexford G. *Grover Cleveland.* New York: Macmillan, 1968.

Welch, Richard E., Jr. *The Presidencies of Grover Cleveland.* Lawrence, KS: University of Kansas Press, 1988.

INDEX

Greeley, Horace, 83, 111, 112
Gresham, Walter, 123, 128
Guam, 150

Harrison, Benjamin, 116, 117,
    128
Havana, 134, 135, 146
Hawaii, 119, annexation of, by
    U.S., 115-116, 121, 123,
    124, 125, 126, 128, 130;
    population of, 115, 122, 123;
    relationship of, with U.S.,
    117, 118, 121, 125, 129, 130,
    132, 132; revolt in, 115, 116,
    118, 120, 121, 122, 124, 128
Hay, John, 114, 150-151
Hudson's Bay Company, 65,
    67, 72

Idaho, 77, 78
impressment, 27, 30, 31, 35,
    40, 41, 45
independence, American, 13,
    16, 18, 30, 32, 33, 35, 37, 45
Independence, Missouri, 76
Indians, 47-50, 69; attitude of
    whites toward, 47, 49, 50-52,
    54, 57, 61; conflict of, with
    white settlers, 47, 50, 51, 58;
    relationship of, with Great
    Britain, 31, 35, 41; U.S.
    policy toward, 47, 48, 50-52,
    55

Jackson, Andrew: and battle of
    New Orleans, 43, 44; and
    nullification, 81-82, 84, 85,
    94; and removal of
    Cherokees from Georgia,
    56, 57-60, 61-62
Japan, 121

Jefferson, Thomas, 32-33, 35,
    38, 69; and purchase of
    Louisiana Territory, 20, 21,
    22, 25-26

Kentucky, 98, 99, 103, 106,
    107
Key, Francis Scott, 42, 43

Lee, Harry, 33
Lewis, Meriwether, 69
Lewis and Clark expedition, 69
Liliuokalani, 115, 118, 121-
    122, 123, 124, 125, 126, 127,
    130, 131, 132
Lincoln, Abraham, 8, 92-93,
    94; election of, 79; and
    emancipation of slaves, 108-
    113, 114
Louisiana (state), 81
Louisiana Purchase, 23, 24, 25,
    26
Louisiana Territory, 12, 23, 24,
    25,

McClellan, George, 103
McKinley, William, 130; and
    Spanish-American War, 146,
    147, 148, 151
Madison, James, 40, 86; and
    War of 1812, 41-42, 45, 46
Maine, USS, 134, 135, 144,
    146, 151
"Manifest Destiny," 65
Marshall, John, 52, 53, 57
Maryland, 98, 103, 107, 114
Mayflower, 96
Mexico, 65, 71, 75
Michigan, 68
militia, state, 32, 38
Mississippi (state), 81

95, 108-109, 111; abolition of, 79, 96, 99, 101-102, 103, 104, 105, 110-114; emancipation of slaves, 104, 105, 106, 107, 109, 111, 112; in border states, 98, 99, 100, 102, 103, 106, 107; history of, in U.S., 96, 97; importance of, in South, 96, 99, 104, 114

Smith, Eldon, 94

smuggling, 12

South Carolina, 81-82, 85, 92, 93; and nullification, 81-82; secession of, 81-82

southern states: attitude of, toward slavery, 79, 80, 82, 87, 96, 98, 99, 104; during Civil War, 95-98, 102, 109; and secession, 81, 82, 83, 84, 85, 86, 91-92, 94, 95, 98, 100

Spain: Cuba controlled by, 133, 134, 135, 136, 137-141, 144, 146, 151; New Orleans controlled by, 10, 11-13, 14, 16, 17-18, 20; and Spanish-American War, 148-150, 151

Spanish-American War, 148, 149, 150-151

"Star Spangled Banner," 42

Stevens, John, 118, 120, 121, 123, 124, 128

sugar plantations, 124, 133

Sumter, Fort, 92-93

Supreme Court, U.S., 52, 53, 54, 57, 62, 101

Ten Years War, 133, 140

Texas, 65, 75, 81

Thirteenth Amendment, 114

Trail of Tears, 59, 60, 62

Turney, Hopkins, 67

Tyler, John, 68, 70, 76

Union, U.S., 79, 83, 87, 88, 90, 111; efforts to preserve, 95, 98, 102, 106, 107, 109, 112, 113; secession of southern states from, 81, 82, 83, 84, 85, 86, 89, 91, 92, 94, 95, 98, 100

Vancouver Island, 70

Virginia, 32, 37, 104, 109

War of 1812, 42-46, 61, 63, 68, 73

Washington (state), 77, 78

Washington, D.C., 42, 43, 98

Washington, George, 6

Welch, Richard, Jr., 132

Weyler, Valeriano, 136

Whigs, 58

White House, 9

Williams, R. Hal, 132

Woodford, Stewart, 139

Woodward, George, 84

Worcester v. Georgia, 52, 57

Photo Credits

Photographs courtesy of The Library of Congress: pp. 6, 8, 21, 24, 25, 31, 34, 40, 43, 44, 53, 56, 61, 69, 73, 80, 83, 91, 92, 96, 108, 110, 113, 116, 117, 119, 122, 138, 139, 143; The Bettmann Archive, 9; Minnesota Historical Society, pp. 15, 22, 29, 37, 70, 74, 89, 100, 102, 104, 112, 127, 140, 142, 147; Oklahoma Historical Society, p. 60; Oregon Historical Society, pp. 66, 76; University of South Carolina, p. 93; Supreme Court Historical Society, p. 101; Hedemann Collection, Bishop Museum, pp. 120, 131; National Archives, pp. 135, 148, 149.

ABOUT THE AUTHOR

NATHAN AASENG is a widely published author of books for young readers. He has covered a diverse range of subjects, including history, biography, social issues, sports, health, business, science, and fiction. Twenty of his books have won awards from organizations such as the national Council for Social Studies, National Science Teachers Association, International Reading Association, Junior Library Guild, and the Child Study Association of America. Aaseng is the author of *Great Justices of the Supreme Court, You Are the President, You Are the Supreme Court Justice, You Are the General,* and the forthcoming book, *America's Third-Party Presidential Candidates.* He lives in Eau Claire, Wisconsin, with his wife and children.